To Nas
celebrate your Soul
every day!
Anna-Louise

The Soul
Whisperer

LIFESUCCESS PUBLISHING, LLC
8900 E Pinnacle Peak Road, Suite D240
Scottsdale, AZ 85255
Telephone: 800.473.7134
Fax: 480.661.1014
E-mail: admin@lifesuccesspublishing.com

ISBN: (soft cover) 978-1-59930-146-4

Cover: Lloyd Arbour & LifeSuccess Publishing
Layout: Fiona Dempsey & LifeSuccess Publishing

COMPANIES, ORGANIZATIONS,
INSTITUTIONS, AND INDUSTRY PUBLICATIONS:
Quantity discounts are available on bulk purchases of this book for reselling, educational
purposes, subscription incentives, gifts, sponsorship, or fundraising. Special books or book
excerpts can also be created to fit specific needs such as private labeling with your logo
on the cover and a message from a VIP printed inside. FOR MORE INFORMATION PLEASE
CONTACT OUR
SPECIAL SALES DEPARTMENT AT LIFESUCCESS PUBLISHING.
Printed by the MPG Books Group in the UK

*All individuals and case notes included herewith have been fictionalised to convey the message
without betraying the identity of participants. Any similarities to individuals, living or dead,
is purely coincidental. All consultations and conversations with clients are held in the strictest
confidence.*

*Disclaimer: The guidance, advice, and suggested visualisations contained within this book are
for enjoyment and inspirational purposes only. No medical opinion is implied in relation to
health, healing, or the causes of ill health. The information contained within this book is in no
way intended to diagnose or replace medical care and attention. If you feel you have a condition of
any nature that requires consultation, examination, or medication, you are encouraged to consult
a physician.*

Anna-Louise Haigh
– *Krisayah Messenger* –

The Soul
Whisperer

Reveals The

Secret Messages

From

Your Soul

DEDICATION

*T*his book is dedicated to the soul that you are and all that you can be.

My soul chose wisely when it aligned with my father, Tom, and my mother, Vonne. Each, in their own way, gave me the seeds of my creativity. They have been my greatest teachers.

My journey so far would have been lacking if it weren't for my brother, Mike, who is my inspiration and mentor. Thank you for being the amazing soul that you are.

ACKNOWLEDGEMENTS

*N*o book writes itself. At the very least it requires inspiration, dedication, love, and commitment from the author if it is worth writing at all.

To facilitate this adventure, there are many supporters and contributors who have helped shape me along the path that has led to the point where I can thank and acknowledge them here.

For all her love and support, I would like to thank Ann Gillanders, who has shown me what can be achieved through self-belief and sheer determination. Eleanor and Geoff Tanner need thanking abundantly, as they have always been willing to listen and guide in the right proportions. My journey has been enriched and nourished by the unconditional love, support and balance provided by Sharon Coleman and it is important that I say a special thanks to her from my heart. Also, to Angela Mahandru, who always lightens my day!

My mentors have been few, yet they have been carefully chosen. They include, along with those mentioned above, Dr Christine Page, Denise Linn, Lita de Alberdi, Tracy Holloway, and Felicity Warner. Each has shared their many lifetimes of wisdom with gentle grace and willingness, for which I thank them most humbly.

I am blessed with a select array of dear close friends and soul sisters, who each generously give of their time, love, humour, clarity, and wisdom, in just the right amounts at just the right time. To the Dandy Hummers, whose presence was determined by divine timing and has enriched my journey, I am blessed to know you. I thank you all most gratefully and am delighted that we are together again in this lifetime.

Special thanks must go to Katy Cox, who has kept me grounded and focused on the days when it was so tempting not to be by having a secret stash of carrot cake at the ready when it was needed most!

Pete Kaufmann deserves a heart felt thank you for his role in helping this book become a reality. He has journeyed with me from the beginning of this project and his contributions and love have taught me a great deal and he will always have a special place in my heart.

Finally, this book would not have been possible without the guidance of Dee Burks, Ray Stoia, Wendy Gallagher, Veronica Marmoreo, the staff at Life Success Publishing, and Morgan James. Your talents and expertise have been invaluable.

TESTIMONIALS

This book will certainly touch your heart and soul with its profound soul whisperings and appreciation of the subtle energies which influence us every day. Written by a gifted intuitive, it weaves together many ways to listen to our inner being, offering sound guidance towards happiness, health and a fulfilment of one's soul purpose.

Dr. Christine Page, mystical physician
and author of *Frontiers of Health*

"On the journey to ultimate freedom, there are times when a guide is an essential 'must have'. Having lost ourselves so many times, it becomes self evident that this is true. Anna-Louise Haigh is such a guide and in *'The Soul Whisperer'* offers a clear, compassionate and easy to follow template for us to reconnect our own 'still small voice within'. Do not lose a moment, read, listen learn and love now, so that you may go on to whisper others into their true being. What a gift. You've earned it..."

Jonathan Louise Trapman, author of
'The Freedom Cycle' – *an epic in Creation*

The Soul Whisperer is a fascinating book to help you connect with your soul and find inner peace.

Nancy Hine, author of
The Depression Trap

'Within the chapters of this timely compendium of soul wisdom, insight and guidance you will find nourishment for your own growth, understanding and reminders of how to live a joy-filled life.'

Jenny Cox, Author - *The Balance Procedure*

We are in a time when many people are searching for answers to the 'big questions' in life. Anna-Louise Haigh, through her unique connection with her authentic higher self, known as Krisayah, bring to light easily readable messages and meanings about life and how to understand the answers to these questions through listening to the whisperings of your soul. You will find yourself within these chapters and emerge enriched and enlightened.

Felicity Warner, founder of The Hospice of the Heart, Soul Midwife and author of *Gentle Dying*

Living life without an awareness of your soul's potential means you are missing out on so much! Through the wealth of information, wisdom and real-life stories provided here, Anna-Louise Haigh brings us the gift of *The Soul Whisperer* so you can start to 'hear' the secret messages your soul has been patiently waiting to reveal. Enjoy this book, you will be forever grateful and your soul will reward you abundantly.

-Bob Proctor, Bestselling author of *You Were Born Rich*

Living life without an awareness of your soul's potential means you are missing out on so much! Through the wealth of information, wisdom and real-life stories provided here, Anna-Louise Haigh brings us the gift of *The Soul Whisperer* so you can start to 'hear' the secret messages your soul has been patiently waiting to reveal. Enjoy this book, you will be forever grateful and your soul will reward you abundantly.-Bob Proctor, Bestselling author of You Were Born RichMaking the decision to acknowledge your inner voice is made easy for you through the insightful and inspirational chapters of *The Soul Whisperer.* Learn how others connected with their souls' messages. Receive the benefit of the soul whisperings that highlight the messages perfectly. This book will awaken a new mindset that will always serve you well.

-Gerry Robert, Bestselling author of
The Millionaire Mindset

Ray Proctor – Living in the modern world brings many challenges, yet there are similarities and themes throughout all our lives. Soul coach Anna-Louise Haigh shows us through the chapters of *The Soul Whisperer* how you can easily start to improve your health, happiness and relationships by connecting with your life purpose.

Following your life purpose is easy. Making the decision to follow it is the hard part! If you have ever wondered why certain patterns or events shadow your life or simply know there is more you can be and yet you haven't hit upon the key that unlocks that door, this book is essential. Clearly written, down-to-earth, practical and positive, Anna-Louise Haigh presents *The Soul Whisperer* as an ideal source of inspiration and information to help you follow your soul's guidance to achieving the life of your dreams.

-Dori J. Locke, Bestselling author of *Results Unlimited*

CONTENTS

WORTH REMEMBERING

There is nothing more real and authentic
than letting your spirit take flight and soar.

When the day comes that you sense a gentle nudge in your heart
and an elbow at your back,
your eyes and heart will look to the skies and remember Home.

This is the moment.

Close your eyes, let your arms lift as though your wings are unfolding
for the very first time.

In a single breath,
feel the tingle of the breeze as you take flight
and play freely among the thermals.

Release. Reconnect. Rejoice.
Remind yourself that you were and always will be an infinite soul
before you were You.

Krisayah

INTRODUCTION

*W*hat makes us want to know more about ourselves? Is it the awareness delivered to us in dreams or coincidences, or through our relationships or misfortunes? What is it that even makes us think that there is more to us than the here and now?

We are all magical beings, and the answers to these questions are nestled within us, surfacing occasionally. If we are 'listening', we seize the opportunity to learn more about ourselves and grow. By tasting only a single drop of this light-filled nectar, we each can experience a life of wonder, joy, and enrichment. We just need to tap into the source – that is the intention of this book.

We all carry within us a life-direction guide, similar to a pre-programmed map for getting through our life by the most enriching, life-enhancing, joy-filled route imaginable. This energy has a voice. It speaks to us in many ways, and yet we are often oblivious to its wisdom and irreverent toward its guidance. However, it unerringly perseveres simply because for as long as we exist, so does its mission for this lifetime.

The guide through which our life unfolds is our soul. It is an energy force that stakes its claim many times over as it seeks to gather all knowledge, learning, and understanding possible about the humanness of being human.

My role is that of a Soul Whisperer. This encompasses the roles of Soul and Past Life Coach, ThetaDNA Practitioner, Intuitive, Mentor, Healer, Midwife to the Dying. I act in service to the soul, supported with over thirty-five years of combined personal and professional experience. I help you find and understand the messages your soul gives through the events in your life, so that these 'whisperings' can speak to your heart and enrich your life accordingly. Along with being a sacred observer to one's growth, I also, when appropriate, receive channeled wisdom intended for guidance and healing on all levels. I have been aware of this gift from a very early age, and until a few years ago I did not consider it 'book worthy', as it was just the norm for me!

Sometimes I look back on my life and consider myself a slow starter. From childhood, I nurtured a deep desire to follow a helping/healing career, which has lead me to this point; I have journeyed nearly five decades on an often challenging, varied, and yet rewarding path. The success others see has been a collaborative result of the learning gained through my own challenges and occasional failure. My journey has been enhanced by my family, who were naturally my first and greatest teachers, and then by those whom I have had the pleasure to meet and work with over the years. Without them – the clients, patients, students, colleagues, and friends – my journey could not have lead to this moment.

WHO IS KRISAYAH?

*T*he process of writing this book has been an amazing journey in itself. My role as a Soul Whisperer and all that it entails has strengthened my connection with my own soul's purpose. Every day, I know I am doing exactly what I am meant to by being in the service of others who want to live the life they were meant to. I am astoundingly grateful for everyone I have encountered along the way. I do not consider myself as having a 'job' or going to 'work' because what I do is who I am! It is my reason for being here at this time.

One of the gifts I have received as each chapter has unfolded is a deeper connection with the presence of what I consider to be a major source of my abilities and the role I am in. From a very early age, I know that I have been aware of one of my past-life selves. I now know that this essence, its character, and its energy is actually me, as my authentic higher self – the embodiment of all I can be.

In my early adolescent years, my soul had tried to bring this awareness to me when I decided to rename myself. The name that felt right and good was Kris. It gave me a fresh start, without any of the baggage and traumas lingering in the background. I felt free, confident, and exhilarated about life. I was soaring high and loving this new me-ness! However, the ruling of a disapproving mother brought me down to earth with a thud, and life got back to how it had been before this brief interlude.

It was not until I was forty-three that the name I resonate with and full vision of this past life existence was revealed to me during a powerful meditation. My previous self was a serene mystic, healer, and seer. She was an Egyptian prophetess – a wise woman with a strong connection to the ancients and the divine. Because of her talents and abilities, she was kept in comfortable imprisonment as the Pharaoh's treasure. She delivered her insights, healing, and wisdom for his benefit alone. I have felt her energy consistently throughout the years, especially when I am working with soul energy. I have sensed her echo in my soul all my life, and yet it has been the process of writing this book that has brought her alive to the fullest extent. This is not a spirit or ghost who visits me. It is very definitely a case of 'same soul, different host'.

During the course of writing this book, I have grown tremendously aware of this energy and I draw on her boundless wisdom and knowledge with ease, as though it is from my own memory and experiences. Now she has her freedom, living as me, which is the source of my elation, enthusiasm, and feelings of sheer bliss, as I live authentically and move through my life, always mindful of the path my soul had chosen to follow. Our shared soul energy is the basis of this book. I have received many whisperings from this elegant yet powerful soul-self. I know I am here in this present life to continue the work that she started so long ago. My parents chose my birth name with care, and I have honoured that for what may be more than half of this life. Now, following a simple yet powerful 'naming ceremony', conducted by Denise Linn a the magical Summerhill Ranch in California, I was....bathed in the sounds of drumming and filled with the love and friendship of some of my soul sisters and brothers, I introduce Krisayah Messenger. The first name was revealed and given to me through a past-life journey a few years ago. The surname originates from my paternal great-grandmother's lineage.

If you have known me as Anna-Louise Haigh, which, for practical reasons, I will continue to use within my career in Complementary Therapies as a Practitioner and Teacher for the time being, then rest assured I am still the same person you have always known. Now though, I am a happier person, living authentically, and able to share even more with those who seek my services. I honour every moment of my past and embrace the potential of the present, knowing that it will create an amazing future.

If you expect anything from this book, listen for your heart resonating with the brief, reflective 'Soul Whisperings'. They speak when there is something meaningful or necessary to say. In addition, allow yourself to absorb the messages from the accounts of the channeled sessions with some of my clients.

Beyond words, let yourself feel the messages and meanings conveyed. Try some of the exercises and affirmations, as they are intended to guide you and strengthen your connection to your soul. Cradle yourself in the palm of your own hands as you tenderly allow yourself to awaken within. Remember, I am a humble soul spokesperson. You hold your own wisdom. Watch for the light arising within you that also radiates from those whose stories are given here, with whom I have shared trust and time. Let your path in life be smoothed and the journey adventuresome. Know that there is light within every cell of your body that radiates like a beacon and shows you the way.

Let the Soul Whisperer speak softly from the source that nourishes your soul....

Anna-Louise Haigh

Krisayah

CHAPTER 1

When Your Soul Calls Your Name

CHAPTER 1

When Your Soul Calls Your Name

Be ever conscious of each new day.
Add a sprinkle of hope and let your dreams guide your way.

Deafening silence. This is the sound of the soul when one's life is caught in a perpetual hamster-wheel-style existence. When the days are uninspiring and indistinguishable, and you find yourself looking in any direction but at the reality of the present instant – and this distraction occupies every waking moment – the soul is muted. What would it take to nudge this infinitely wise master from its enforced silence? It is only when we are on a collision course with ourselves that the soul releases a desperate scream [which] echoes in some quarter of our lives in an attempt to attract our attention and avoid disaster.

Since this force is so strong within us, perhaps we should be properly introduced!

Stilling myself in readiness for some insight, it wasn't long before I was aware of the familiar voice from deep within. This is how one's soul makes its introduction. My sense of wonder wanted to know, 'What is the soul?' The reply began slowly and almost tempered itself to ensure that I was following and absorbing the words. Enjoying my solitude and the comfort of this connection, the whisperings began:

I am speaking to you as the wisdom of your soul. While you may come to understand and learn the gifts of this infinite sage, it is impossible to truly know me, as I am an elusive and evolving life force. I am an energy that exists both before and after the life of its human host – you. Each person is made up of their soul and their spirit. It is the spirit of the person that expresses itself through their character. From this union, a complex personality begins to develop after birth that will continue to mature throughout the lifetime of the individual.

As your guide for this lifetime, I know you, and grow with you through your experiences.

I embrace and care for you through your heart. I forgive and thank you for every opportunity to grow. Through the fulfillment of your ambitions you honour me.

We travel together. The person you know yourself to be, your spirit, and I are on an incredible journey of exploration and adventure. We are one. We are all you need for this lifetime; there is no other way. I am a spark of the divine. I am unconditional love, and therefore so are you. I am your inner wisdom. I am your soul! We journey together through this lifetime and help each other grow. Thank you for allowing me to experience this growth through you.

25

When you awaken to my wise voice, you begin a journey towards a profusion of knowledge that will lead to the most abundantly wealthy life you could ever imagine. Acknowledging and honouring your soul neither requires nor contradicts religious definition, belief, or comfort. The evidence of the existence of the soul is universal and timeless. As a human host, you've undertaken a journey without an earthly destination that nonetheless has a definite route that is determined one lifetime at a time.

What do you really know about yourself? Have you asked yourself lately? Whenever you still yourself and listen to the voice that whispers from within, you are experiencing a self-defining moment. I thank you for your willingness to listen.

Have you heard your soul call your name lately? How would you recognise it?

I often work with clients who find themselves at a turning point, facing personal and spiritual challenges and even collapse, recovering from crises or illness, and generally trying to find their value and path in this life. They have found themselves, as perhaps you have, seeking the answers to the 'big questions' in life. As a Soul Whisperer and coach, I am a guide and a mentor in service to the soul. I do not give the answers.

SOUL WHISPERING

Wisdom involves listening to your heart, speaking with your inner voice, hearing with compassion, and being in touch with your soul.

*S*o often, although many 'boxes' in our lives may be ticked when the status quo is comfortable and not too challenging, the soul nudges us and says through our heart, 'There has to be more to life than this!' Many people experience this at a time when life is unfulfilling or challenging. For some, this comes when they think life should be getting easier. This usually begins to happen when one's career is established, home and family are sorted, finances are stable, and one's responsibilities are well managed. It's not a question of boredom. At this stage, one has just finally run out of excuses that have kept them from previously listening to the call of their soul.

Some call this a mid-life crisis. In reality, it can happen at any age. What is common is that instead of looking within to find answers, most people traditionally try to find answers from the external means around them. In reality, the potential for everything they want is already inside them. Love, health, abundance, security, hope, joy, and contentment are all waiting within the soul for recognition. People come to realise that material wealth and the possessions they buy always have a shelf life, and the latest 'must have' is only desirable until the next thing comes along. All of this brings limited satisfaction, as the person who they are trying to be is also an illusion. Caught up in a world of 'make-you-believe' they embrace the latest trends as their gods, hoping that a hot designer label will act as guardian angel.

People have moved house, have renovated or bought second and third homes, divorced, remarried, had affairs, had babies, travelled, adopted outrageous diets or extreme lifestyles, joined diverse groups and organisations, or taken up all-consuming hobbies. Basically, they have distracted themselves from trying to find what their life truly has to offer them by chasing one media-generated fantasy or another that presumes to tell them how their life should be. In the process, because they can never quite obtain that illusive carrot dangled before them, they believe that they are a failure if their life, body, partner, home, career, and bank balance doesn't match the projected image of desirability.

If you are reading closely, you will have noticed that there is a glimmer of hope in all of this. I did say, until recently, that this has been the traditional way of life!

Now, more than ever before in our evolution, we are free to release ourselves from our soul's slumber and start to make our own choices from the heart. The traditional life plan of getting married and having children before one's mid-twenties is rarely followed these days. It is also fast becoming an outmoded way of thinking that we must work for several decades, in a career that operates around us rather than emanating from us, spending the last ten to fifteen of those years counting down the days. Single parenting, marrying late if at all, early retirement, career breaks, and creative job sharing all mean that whether we realise it or not, the soul is speaking to a new generation of emerging wise ones and the trend is growing.

SOUL WHISPERING

Nothing is as strong as the spirit - no matter how delicate or colourful the exterior. Think of the fragile butterfly, which can migrate thousands of miles each year.

*P*artly due to the success of the Internet, there is so much more information available now to help build a soul-nourishing spiritual life that really works in the real world. In addition, books, courses, evening classes, retreats, study holidays to spiritually significant places, traditional wisdoms being used as company policy, and A-list actors making films with a spiritual message are all indications of the growing positive tide of awakening humanity.

We know that the planet is sick. Both humanity and Mother Earth need a great amount of repair and support. By questioning our motives for the pursuit of wealth and material abundance, we are guided to honour our inner worth. We are listening to the call of our soul.

Yes, there will always be those who guide their lives by external measures. This provides a necessary balance. These may well include young souls needing to experience this type of life by choice so that in later incarnations, other, more soul-nurturing pursuits can be explored.

To be clear, I believe that it is possible to 'have it all' – the house, the partner, the bulging bank account, the high-flying career, jewels, cars, boats, jet planes, and whatever else you can think of. In reality, none of these things are in themselves good or bad, right or wrong. However, the essential question is: why do you want these things? Ask yourself that the next time you are considering a purchase worth more than ten per cent of your yearly, monthly, or even weekly earnings. What are you going to gain or attract by acquiring this latest purchase? If the answer is an ego-rush and a daydream of the head-turning power of this item, then you are not living from a soul perspective – your soul is not directing you to make this purchase or perform this action. Make your purchase if you so desire, but do it in spite of how others view you for having it, and enjoy it for the sheer joy it will bring you.

Some people feel genuinely guided to make significant changes in their life, and realise that this may generate a period of great unrest involving emotional challenge, discomfort, and even pain for others around them. This is a quite different situation than allowing your frustration to manifest itself in ways that are selfish and harmful to others, merely because you cannot communicate it any other way.

SOUL WHISPERING

Live in the knowledge that emergence need not bring emergency.

*P*erhaps you have had a glimmer of your soul calling to you. This might have been when you wanted to follow a heart-felt ambition or life path, but for whatever reason you didn't. Because the flame of this ambition still flickers quietly within you, you simply know that your life is not on track. You do know, however, that there is something out there with your name on it, just waiting for you, and that when you connect with it, your life will make sense and you will know what you are here for. Perhaps you need to create a blueprint of your life to gain some clarity and motivation.

Many people experience repeated events or circumstances in their life and wonder why they can't break the pattern. These may include bad relationships, bosses who never appreciate them, children who never call, or perpetual financial problems. Through these, your soul calls to you to awaken to the lessons to be learned so that you can grow.

Some start to hear the whisperings from their soul as they daydream to escape some uncomfortable, presently challenging reality. They often gaze at the sky, watching the clouds drift by on a background of softest blue, connecting the soul to its divine origins in the eternal dimension where souls reside between lives, beyond our magnificent planet. This skyward linking can often carry feelings similar to that of a 'homecoming' when the connection is made. During these times, this activity opens our 'thinking mind' and our spiritual heart that then yields questions and insights about our present life and how the future might be better. If you listen closely, you will discover what this life is all about.

SOUL WHISPERING

When your soul rekindles learning from previous lives, the undeniable feelings of 'homecoming' fill your heart and radiate from you in swells of tangible joy.

*E*qually, when life seems unfair, and our heavy, negative feelings govern us – when we are challenged or burdened – we look to the natural environment around us and study the ground, eyes firmly locked downward, as we aimlessly fire our emotionally charged bullets. When we need to heal emotionally and cleanse our soul, we find such solace associated with water, whether it is under the shower or in a long hot bath, as we allow its constant motion to soothe our tattered heart. Wherever your soul directs you, know that this little voice is ultimately waiting to lovingly guide you out of the troubled times and carry you through the rest of your life.

SOUL WHISPERING

Take notice of something that catches your eye; you were meant to see it.

*S*o, has your soul called your name lately? Maybe you just haven't recognised it. The following is inspiration I received when pondering how this might come about:

'How does a soul communicate?' I asked. I was quickly answered.

The soul is constantly willing to communicate; however you have to listen. To your heart, to your inner wisdom, to your intuition, to your health, to the dreams you have at night, to the flashes of inspiration and wisdom that seem to come from nowhere, to the knowledge you hold without knowing where it comes from, to the events around you, and the relationships you form. Then ask, 'Am I paying attention to the messages from these most knowledgeable of guides?' If not, you may find yourself struggling in one or more of these domains. You may wander from the path and experience similar circumstances repeatedly, until you 'hear' the guidance from your soul.

There are hundreds of examples. No doubt you will have some of your own. The soul often speaks to us through what people call 'luck'. A sign that we are following our path, whether through conscious decision and action or not, is that life flows effortlessly.

We meet the right people in the right place at the right time. We 'shine', as our health radiates a noticeable glow. Our relationships, although not always without differences of opinion, are totally supportive and nurturing, and allow us to truly be ourselves as we give and receive love unconditionally. Even though we are aware of the big picture, we remember that the little things matter most. The purity of the soul expresses itself in random acts of kindness. It inspires you to be creative – whether in everyday tasks or actually producing something that says, 'this is me, right now!' We live a joy-filled life of our own making, and pursue our ambitions with confidence, in the belief that we can truly have anything we desire in life.

This may sound like an unobtainable, sugar-coated dream. If it does, or if you can think of someone who never seems get a lucky break and whose life is filled with challenges, then perhaps the soul has been silenced for too long.

Some definite signs of this include: feeling unfulfilled in one's career or relationships; being restless without knowing why or what should be changed to make life better; perpetuating patterns of self-damaging or self-denying behaviour (such as addictions, workaholism, feeling miserable, dejected, and begrudging toward others when they have something good happen). Also, continued minor health problems or major illness are huge wake-up calls from the soul.

The evidence continues and touches every part of one's life and life becomes a struggle. The crimes against the soul make grim reading. Without considering that there may be another way, responding negatively or aggressively to everything shows the disharmony in play. Other examples include: acting against one's own best interests regarding the type of partners or relationships one forms, allowing mental confusion to manifest as physical clutter, poorly defined boundaries about how personal time and energy are spent, being forever in debt through wild financial abandon, and finally, a deep lack of self-confidence and self-esteem, which so often leads to self-sabotage even though success is just within reach.

You will recognize the call of your soul as a feeling.

It is to be hoped that the average person has not experienced too many burdensome 'soul callings' before waking to the patterns and opportunities that are beckoning.

33

With myriad opportunities for the soul to express itself and catch our attention, many people miss that first glimmer of contact and need a few clues in order to recognise it properly.

Does that sound familiar? You will recognize the call of your soul as a feeling. It starts in your heart and feels like a balloon filling with air or an energy swell. And when your heart can't contain it any longer, it fills your chest and may even cause you to raise your arms as though they were beautiful wings just waiting for the breeze to take hold and gently lift you skywards to soar in total, blissful freedom. It brings joy, elation, euphoria, and a sense of unlimited potential just waiting to be released.

Take a moment and think of an occasion or time when everything seemed absolutely right in your world – a time when you secretly wished that things would never change. What do you see, smell, hear, taste, and touch? Let your senses make this moment as real as it was initially. Close your eyes and take yourself there now, for as long as you want.

If you feel that you have not yet had a magical, soul-connecting experience, close your eyes and imagine what it would take to generate these feelings. When you are ready, open your eyes. How did that feel? Write down your feelings if it helps to anchor the experience. What would it be like if nearly every day felt that way? It can happen when you learn to listen to your soul and trust its guidance.

Your soul also talks to you in the language of intuition and gives you a sense of 'knowing' something without consciously registering it prior to your awareness. This is called claircognisance – knowing without knowing.

How many times have you simply 'known' something but not understood where the knowledge originated from? When was the last time that words of wisdom released themselves from your mouth before they registered in your consciousness? This is a strong sign that your soul is talking both to you and through you! All too often we are tempted to hush its whispering voice in favour of what may seem like safer, or more logical or desirable actions and decisions, only to realise afterwards that had we listened, we would have been more enriched and enlightened. Thankfully, the soul is not a quitter! It will try and try again until it earns your trust and you benefit in kind.

In my own life, I began responding to the calls of the soul very much by chance at about the age of ten. My parents were quite surprised and relieved that I handled the news of their divorce so calmly, though I had 'known' for months before they announced it. I was just glad that they had finally said something! What struck me, though, was how I 'knew' it was going to happen, since there were no apparent signs.

This was one of my earliest memories of being aware of my psychic sensitivity. However, I realised that I was sensing the disharmony in their souls. Life needed to change for them, and they bravely honoured their inner guidance. They had done their job of jointly hosting my brother and I to a point when the timing was right, and their separation was a necessary step for the next phase of growth to begin for all of us.

SOUL WHISPERING

Trust in your inner voice. It speaks to you of lifetimes of knowledge gathered specifically to help you in this moment.

*I*f I had had the vocabulary when I first experienced it, I would have perhaps recognised my calling many years ago. Introduced to the mysteries of the Ouija board at the age of eleven, I felt an awakening within me that resonated with familiarity as I was increasingly reminded of the forces and energy beyond the physical reality of daily life.

This is what makes me, as others describe it, a highly intuitive soul whisperer.

Although my mother and I were in awe of this seemingly innocent parlour 'game', the Ouija board quickly doomed itself to the bonfire for being far too spooky and terrifyingly accurate. 'I bet it didn't see that coming!' I thought as the hungry fire began to consume the over-enthusiastic oracle, which emitted peacock-coloured flames in protest. However, this brief encounter rekindled my interest in 'messages from within'.

My abilities do not make me a medium, because I do not aim to connect with the deceased. However, I do work closely with the 'spirit' of my client, acting as a bridge between the inner world of the soul and the outer world of our existence and ambitions. This is what makes me, as others describe it, a highly intuitive soul whisperer. In reality, you too can be your own Soul Whisperer. You have the gifts already within you; with guidance and practice, you can connect with this wisdom. As you read the chapters that follow, my aim is to help you achieve this connection.

Like you, there are days when I am less sparkly than others; of course there are – this is part of being human. However, these times serve as reminders and motivate one to reconnect with the inner well of joy that fuels everything.

On many occasions during my early adolescence, I would go alone into nature – the place I felt most comfortable and carefree – when life got to be too much and my emotions needed untangling. I would walk in the woodlands and near rivers, or sit by the lake in front of our house, where I could relax. Even though I was still quite young, I was well aware of the internal, driving forces that are intended to guide me and impart wisdom.

As I would silently ask myself questions during my time in my natural playground, I would almost always receive a rapid response. I now know that these were healing messages spoken softly by my soul that were intended to guide, reassure, comfort, and illuminate. I always found my solace here.

These whisperings are now a constant presence in my life. Although I did not fully appreciate or understand this initially, for the purposes of learning, healing, and living an inspired, blissful life, I now converse regularly with my soul. When it calls, I listen.

From the moment the heart swells with energy from the soul and embraces the spark of the divine within itself, it responds by sounding the first beat of its lifelong rhythm. The soul is waiting to share its knowledge and to learn what it came to Earth this time around. It is here, in the infinity between each heartbeat that the soul speaks. This is why so many hosts cannot make or keep the connection – they simply do not still themselves often enough, if ever, to listen to the wisdom within that can be accessed through the soul.

Let me explain how to make the connection with your soul. Try this method for five minutes each day, or even five minutes per week, and see how you feel after several attempts. Find a warm, safe, and quite comfortable place where you will not be disturbed. Try to sit, as lying down is too conducive to drowsiness. Have a pen and notepad beside you, perhaps with a couple of questions you wish to find the answers to written in it, with space below each question to record any insights you might receive. Focus on your breathing. If your mind begins to chatter, thank it for its concern and ask it to wait its turn. When your mind is still, ask your first question and meditate quietly, waiting for the answer. It will probably come in your own voice. Do not question the message or the words you receive. Simply write down what you receive and ask your next question. Just imagine what you could learn from this exercise. Try it, and open the doors to this magical chamber.

Do not feel that you have wasted your time if you do not immediately receive a response. This can happen for a number of reasons. You might have received a response but instantly dismissed it. You may also be trying too hard to obtain a specific response, the one that you would like to receive, rather than the one your soul wants to give. Or, perhaps, you simply were not meant to receive an answer during this attempt. Don't give up. Try asking different questions, at different times of the day, in different locations.

Your soul will only ever give you information that is for your ultimate good, which means also that the answers must come at the right time. The information you receive is for you to act or reflect upon as part of your own personal growth and development. For this reason, it is no use to ask for the winning lottery numbers, as the effects of such a windfall may obstruct the soul's path and not, ultimately, improve one's life.

Often, the soul speaks symbolically to us through our dreams – day or night. One need not be an expert on symbology to interpret these messages. If the meaning is not immediately obvious, quiet your mind and ask your soul what the symbol is meant to represent.

With practice, you will be able to check in with your soul anywhere, at anytime, regarding anything! Honouring your soul, then, becomes your key to the kingdom of miracles, as your life begins to unfold rather than unravel in the most spectacular way.

CHAPTER 2

Universoul Language

CHAPTER 2

Universoul Language

*When your soul speaks to you, it guides you
with unconditional love along the course that will be
for your highest good. Learn the soul's vocabulary
and start to converse fully.*

*W*hen we embark on the search for life's greater personal meaning, we need a spiritual toolbox filled with the proper tools to enable us to build the life we desire. Some of the necessary tools include: setting aside time for personal reflection and meditation, and keeping a journal documenting your growth, ambitions, and inspirational thoughts. You may also wish to find a spiritual teacher with whom you are in tune, and who can offer guidance and opportunities for growth.

So that we can fully understand the present vocabulary and be able to speak in clearer terms, we need to have a basic understanding of the terminology commonly used regarding spirituality and the progression of the soul. Obviously, a subject as vast and ever expanding as the development of the spirit and soul, there will inevitably be some disagreement over terms. Do not let this confuse or dishearten you.

SOUL WHISPERING

The language of the soul is universal.
Listen to your heart and be as your soul.

*T*here are many ways of interpreting and discussing the energy that defines and guides us. The understanding of these terms and concepts should not be clouded for the sake of a dictionary definition. There are two facts here that are quite relevant.

First, every journey begins someplace. If you have found this book early in your quest for personal knowledge, let what follows serve as a foundation. However, it is important to always be open and willing to seriously consider other people's views and descriptions of their experiences, knowledge, and understanding.

Second, if you have already begun your journey and discovered more about your life potential through a greater understanding of your soul, welcome new insights and evaluate whether they resonate with your own inner experience. If they do, great! If not, simply let them slip by. Regardless, continue reading and look for truths that will enable you to engender a deeper soul consciousness.

Let us begin our discussion of terms by asking: What is the Spiritual Trinity? What is the difference between your soul and your spirit? Do you know your higher or soul purpose? Are you on a soul journey or undergoing spiritual discovery? Where does your soul path lead? Are you working for your highest good or your higher self?

These questions all contain terms that are commonly used to describe the journey of discovering your authentic self and attaining life enrichment. They are all components of a spiritual life quest. Understanding these terms will allow you to get on with the main feature – the journey!

SOUL WHISPERING

There is no destination, just the adventure of the journey. If you think you have arrived, you have not begun.

*T*he Spiritual Trinity is made up of the soul, which is the energy that unites with successive physical hosts over many lifetimes, the spirit, which gives expression to the qualities of the soul, and the higher self, which is the ultimate potential of all that we can be – usually manifested when we learn to listen to our soul wisdom and follow its guidance. Through a delicate balance they are interlinked and interdependent. They co-operate through shared wisdom and strengths, and yet each plays a different role in guiding our development. Their synergy creates the guiding force that provides us with infinite opportunities to live as our soul intended.

To embrace the Spiritual Trinity, it is best to have a familiarity with these terms. To begin with, we know that each person hosts a soul, which is the first component of the trinity.

The soul is, understandably, quite an elusive concept to clearly describe. Most people accept or feel that all things have a source – a Creator. Regardless of the name assigned to this Creator, its omnipresent force is still evident. The soul, then, is an extension and reflection of this creative energy.

Similar to the concept of angels, the soul is non-denominational. It simply is. Most people have heard the terms 'spirit' and 'soul' in connection with religion. However, when we talk about the soul and spiritual development in today's rapidly emerging soulistically aware culture, it is in terms of examining our full life potential by acknowledging and utilising our inborn wisdom, which is intended to safely guide us. Both the religious and spiritual, non-denominational views of the soul can coexist harmoniously within your own daily life, and your life will be enriched if you let them.

Exploring the gifts of the soul is a personal pursuit that focuses inwardly rather than looking for answers from an external source. There is no reason why a personal journey cannot exist in tandem with a strong, well-established belief system. The essences of each are complementary, in that both approaches seek to provide a person the best life possible through the most appropriate means.

SOUL WHISPERING

The language of the soul speaks through the heart. It does not require alignment with categories, casts, or cultures.

*T*he psychic and religious views of the soul differ in that the former, as I have always believed, teaches that we carry our 'church' within us. In other words, it is possible to connect with the essence of the divine anytime and anywhere. Thus, it is possible to make every moment of every day a deeply connected spiritual experience. This is achievable because the soul is a direct reflection of an all-powerful and loving creative source. Therefore, when we seek to connect with this divine spark and understand the Tao, or Way of the Soul, we naturally begin to live as we are intended to. When we learn to listen to the messages from the soul and connect with them at any time, we can then draw on them as a source of inspiration, guidance, reassurance, and healing.

The soul has its own agenda for each lifetime. Although it comes to Earth to learn, it brings with it the wisdom it has gleaned from its previous incarnations. I sense it as a linear energy moving progressively forward. The trauma of birth removes many of these memories from our consciousness. In some ways, this is quite beneficial to us. Imagine what life would be like if we consciously remembered all our previous incarnations, deeds, relationships, trials, and traumas? This would make our current life total chaos. Instead, these memories are held within the soul and are used as to guide us and give us strength and wisdom when we need it.

It is fair to say that during each previous life, our soul will have gained some knowledge, redeemed and accumulated some karma, made vows that will perhaps influence our present life, and created soul contacts with which we reunite through different lifetimes and in different relationships. Naturally, some of our soul's lives will have been mundane. Others will have been rife with hardship and strife. Still others will have been more comfortable and leisurely. Not every soul was rich and famous at some point!

SOUL WHISPERING

*Honour your journey; it was determined long
before you took your first step.*

*A*s souls continually advance through reincarnation, they experience all sorts of enriching experiences and challenges that increase their knowledge, wisdom, and understanding. It is possible for an old wise soul to be hosted by a child; one can sense this, even in an infant, by looking into its eyes. It is likely that the younger people of today host more mature souls than the generations before them. Many under 30 have grown up in a world full of possibilities and privileges, with access to so much information via the Internet. Most people under the age of 40 living in the West have experienced no real suffering or deprivation. Fewer people alive today have suffered the restrictions and realities of war, famine, or the fight for survival. They intuitively know about these things so well because of their soul's evolution that they do not have to learn lessons through hardship, loss, hard work, pain, and suffering in the way that previous generations had to, so they can now spend their time making life work for them! They pursue fun, fame, and fortune, probably because their souls lack sufficient experience with these things. Perhaps we could learn from them and cast off the ingrained heritage of 'work hard to pay the bills' handed down to us by earlier generations.

Although most of our memories and psychic wisdom from previous lives are left behind at the gateway of birth, we do retain a certain amount. From them, we are able to develop our individual talents, character, preferences, and so forth, all of which are continually enhanced throughout our lifetimes. We reconnect with this accumulated knowledge and innate wisdom, and update it in our time between lives, where souls gather and rest in preparation for their next hosting.

When we are born, our skulls are not fully formed. This allows the plates of the skull to flex, making it possible for babies to pass through the birth canal. There are several places, called fontanels, where the plates of the infant's skull do not meet. These areas are covered only with skin and a tough membrane until the bones grow together. The main fontanel is located at the top of the head, immediately above the Crown Chakra, one of the body's seven major energy centres according to Eastern traditions. These traditions teach that we connect with the universe through the Crown Chakra.

It is most common during early years, when this fontanel is still open, for children to speak about their previous lives. At a very young age, children will often display artistic talents far beyond their years, or speak beyond their years, even though, understandably, we believe that they lack the necessary life experience to account for such mature thinking. By the time one reaches the 'terrible two's' – the time when a child's behaviour can be most challenging – the plates of the skull have fused, not only forming a strong encasement for the brain, but also creating a barrier that restricts continued free-flowing connection with the universe.

Is it possible that the behaviour changes witnessed in the youngster are a reflection of the significance and impact of this diminished connection with energy from the universe? After this stage, our memories of past lives slowly dwindle as we learn about life from our parents and others around us. Children become conditioned to life through their experiences and views. Any remnants of the soul memories are usually surrendered by the time they have been in formal education for a couple of years. There are numerous accounts of young children, usually under the age of seven, who can recall exact details about their previous times on earth. Some even appear to have returned to the same family and can recall events from several generations earlier. The tradition of finding the next Dalai Lama is based on this very possibility.

SOUL WHISPERING

*Study your dreams when the night-time calls,
and messages from behind the veil will impress
upon you.*

The purpose of submerging most of our prior knowledge is to leave us more readily available to learn the lessons of this lifetime. However, our natural talents will represent a strong driving force within us that is undeniable. We see this as 'raw talent' in many musicians, artists, actors, sculptors, and writers. The reason that the soul expresses its accumulated talents through the creative arts is that this wondrous energy source expresses itself through creativity. This is what brings true joy, and connects us with our soul. The next time you see a musician or performing artist passionately engaged in their art, watch their face. You will see the soul connectedness and feel their energy resounding with the sheer magnificence of being as their soul intended. They are expressive, creative, passionate, appreciated, uplifted, and gratuitously sharing their gifts.

A soul knows and understands the life it is uniting with, and because of this, it may be reluctant to venture into it! In some cases, this is seen when a child is particularly difficult or unruly, or when an adult is a daydreamer without any sense of grounding or urgency. Because the soul is a highly vibrating, radiant being, its signature is light filled, loving, and wise. Humans vibrate at a much slower frequency when we take on physical form, and therefore become anchored to the planet. For a soul, it takes a bit of time to become grounded and familiar with the concept of having a body, including how to use and care for it! To have a successful earthly experience, it must balance itself between the roles of a being a soul and being human.

The seeds of wisdom are anchored deep within us, and surface when we connect with the inner wisdom our soul has to share. This can be successfully achieved by working with a soul coach and mentor, such as myself, who specializes in connecting you with your soul's wisdom and learning its messages whether for physical, emotional, or mental healing, or for personal growth and life enrichment.

SOUL WHISPERING

We come from the light as a divine spark, and
we return to the light as a divine spark. It is
the journey in between that is enriching.

*W*hen the end of life is near, the soul may signal to its host so that they are able to make a better transition. Although the person may not consciously 'know' what will soon happen, they may feel the need to say special good-byes and be with the people they treasure the most. In cases of sudden, tragic, or totally unexpected death, the soul may leave the person a few days earlier to avoid experiencing the pain. It often lingers nearby in an act of caring and reassurance.

Upon dying, the soul leaves the body through the Crown Chakra and returns to its own kingdom to review and share what it's most recently learned, so that all members of its soul family can benefit and progress and grow together, and make preparations for the next life. The timing between visits may be short, or it may last several generations in human terms. The soul decides when to return and for what reason. It does not, however, decide how it is to depart. The rest plays out as the life unfolds!

The spirit is different from the soul, yet these words are often used interchangeably, so it can get a bit confusing. The spirit is often called the 'essence' of the person. It is their innate nature, general personality, and approach to life, as well as their memorable and enduring character. The spirit is like the perfume of a flower – invisible, yet of a distinct character. It is what lingers in your memory when the physical person is not present. The spirit frees itself from the body after death and is meant to then make its way back to the spirit world. Often, the spirit will linger near the deceased's relatives and friends for a while to make sure they are going to be all right.

After the spirit has left the body it retains an imprint of its human counterpart

In some cases, the spirit may try to express itself or make its presence known by temporarily taking on an animal form – such as a dove or butterfly, or through a family pet – just so they can be closer to their loved ones for a while. After the spirit has left the body, it retains an imprint of its human counterpart that many talented mediums are able to connect with and transfer accurate personal messages to and from. It is the spirit that can become trapped between worlds when its transition has not been complete for some reason. In such cases, assistance from a trusted source may be necessary to guide it on its way.

While there is a strong argument that every living thing has a soul, it is the spirit that can re-enter the three-dimensional physical world as a member of the animal and mammal kingdom. This could be why people attribute human characteristics to animals – in particular cats, dogs, horses, and even dolphins. Often pets arrive in our lives to bring certain gifts that they were not able to display as a human spirit, such as unconditional love, playfulness, freedom, comfort through touch, or protection. Our pets may even choose us because their spirit has something it wants to share or nurture within us.

Every one of us has both a soul and a spirit. The soul aligns with the spirit to form a symbiotic relationship for the duration of the host's life.

So far, we have described two of the three components of the Spiritual Trinity. The third aspect is called the higher self. This component is the ultimate personification of the most positive, happy, content, fulfilled, creative, loving, and caring attributes of yourself that you can imagine. You will recognise it through definite feelings that register in your heart as a sense of elation, wholeness, bliss, or being filled with love. The higher self is the vision of the person you aspire to be in this lifetime.

SOUL WHISPERING

Turn your eyes skyward and think of home.

*Y*our higher self is a guiding force. When you act in accordance with it, your endeavours will be in alignment with your soul's best interests. Your higher self embraces your ultimate potential, supported by the many lifetimes of learning, knowledge, and growth you've already experienced.

Naturally, because we are all human beings with free will, there will be times when we do not act in our best interest. The decisions you make now about your behaviour, responses, and dealings with others reflect whether you are following your vision of your higher self.

To explain it another way, in order to achieve a state of being as your higher self, you need to adopt a principal of always acting in your highest good. This is achieved by not saying or doing anything that would be to your detriment. You've heard phrases such as, 'I think it is in my best interest to' or 'I feel it would serve me well if '. What these phrases are really saying is, 'I want to act for my highest good' or 'I am taking this course of action because I feel it is in my highest good'. This doesn't mean that someone is making decisions selfishly, for their benefit alone. What we are saying, whether we realise it or not, is that our vision of ourselves as our higher self is achieved through acting for our highest good.

If you act for your highest good, you will not behave in certain ways, or make decisions that harm you in some way. This means that your motivation behind a course of action or the desired outcome reflects the person you would like to become. Ultimately, we should all strive to always act in our highest good. Can you imagine how life would be if this were the norm for everyone?

We are here to learn. Mistakes and challenges are inevitable, otherwise our soul would not have the opportunities to grow that it seeks. It is how we respond to things and what we learn that determines how our soul progresses. When faced with difficult decisions, challenges, or trying times, it helps to centre yourself and ask inwardly, 'What course of action is in my highest good or reflects my higher self in this circumstance?' Listen for the reply and trust its source, and then act upon it.

SOUL WHISPERING

Imagine how wonderfully nurturing life will be
when you live by the guidance of your soul.

*B*y genuinely asking for wisdom from the heart, you will never be guided wrongly because the soul is the reflection of the divine within you. It is the harmonious balance between of each of these three aspects that comprises what I call 'soulistic empowerment'. Neither is regal over another. It is their synergy that impels one's life towards greater wisdom and wholeness, and ultimately furthers our soul's enrichment. The soul and spirit collaborate to guide you, with the help of the influence and vision of your higher self – powered by acting in your highest good – so that you move along your soul purpose for this lifetime.

Many people get up each morning, go about their daily routine, perform their responsibilities, go to bed, and get up the next day and for the rest of their life without wondering what more life could offer them. It is only at times when our soul tries to catch our attention, perhaps during a particularly low emotional period, or when we feel in a rut, that we declare, 'There has to be more to life than this!' or we ask, pleadingly into the vast emptiness, 'What is my life all about?'

A developing soul will choose hundreds if not thousands of human hosts, sometimes with long respites between attachments until it has learned the vast qualities and experiences of the humanness of being human. On each linking, there is a pre-determined contract or soul purpose for its time in that particular body.

Your soul purpose is basically the contract of experience and learning a soul agrees to prior to choosing you as its host. When we follow a life path that honours our soul purpose, we feel supported. Although there may be learning opportunities that present themselves as challenges, losses, hardship, and adversity, there is an unerring presence that gives us strength from our soul that helps us to carry on. This is one of the gifts the soul gives as it supports you during the hard times and directs you toward recognising life's lessons when they come. Ultimately, this can lead to a life of enrichment.

The soul's journey, however, is a larger concept. This journey spans the full duration of experience over many lifetimes that your soul requires in order to gain the learning and knowledge it needs. It is understood that when the soul reaches the point where the majority of its karma is cleared, ascension is possible. At this point, the soul becomes enlightened and can then choose how best to serve all humanity. Some souls elect to stay on the planet to work more closely with individuals or communities, while others leave their physical body and occupy a place in the spiritual hierarchy that oversees all life. As a Certified Soul Coach, I initiate a connection for my clients to explore their inner world by guiding them on either a Soul Journey or a Past Life Journey experience. This incredibly powerful and transformative process allows the client to find answers that are held within their soul, release blockages, conquer fears, manifest their potential, and ultimately create the life and future they desire through utilising this deep connection with the truth that their soul holds.

> *Your soul fulfils its purpose as it continues along its journey by following its soul path.*

Your soul fulfils its purpose as it continues along its journey by following its soul path. This is the route the soul will take to get from A to B, from this life to the next, and on throughout all its lives. The path is its map across many lifetimes.

Finally, to ensure that we continue to seek life enrichment and soul empowerment, we must consciously engage in the process of always focusing on our higher purpose. This means that we never lose sight of our soul's quest, the journey we are personally on, and the path we choose to follow. Acting for your higher purpose ensures that all other dimensions of the spiritual seeker's journey and the Spiritual Trinity are fulfilled.

CHAPTER 3

Awakening Your Heart Centres

CHAPTER 3

Awakening Your Heart Centres

We are all sparks of divine light radiating from deep within.

*W*e all want to be assured that we are lovable and loved. This is one of the basic essentials to helping create well-balanced individuals who can contribute and participate fully in life. Of all the experiences a soul might need to undergo and learn from, establishing a solid foundation of love, which is ideally unconditional, is commonly one of the main goals in each lifetime.

One of the reasons for the presence of the soul is to learn through your experiences and in return to guide your life based on understanding unconditional love. It is hardly surprising that our emotions govern not only our heart's health but the health of our whole body as well, because this is the barometer by which we tell how closely aligned we are with our soul purpose or soul path.

SOUL WHISPERING

When you listen to your heart,
your life begins to flow.

*I*t has long been known in Eastern traditions that we house a series of swirling energy centres within, above, and below the body. There are seven main energy centres that align with the main hormonal glands in the body, beginning at the base of the spine and ascending past the throat to the centre of the brow, finally ending at the crown of the head. These energy centres are called chakras, which in Sanskrit means 'wheel'. Imagine that from the base of your spine to the top of your head these seven vortices each radiates its own colour and energy vibration.

Emotions are a form of energy, and each chakra resonates with the vibration of certain emotions. When we experience strong feelings that have an impact on our thinking or behaviour, the energy of that emotion is drawn into the vortex of the chakra. If the emotions are present long enough and strongly enough, they start to accumulate and can cause disharmony that may eventually affect the surrounding organs and hormonal glands, causing disease. Most often, it is not until we experience physical symptoms that we realise that something is out of balance in our body. All too often, we immediately resort to drugs and even surgery to deal with the inconvenience of illness. However, if we looked at the state of our energy, particularly in our heart centre we may be able to treat the cause of our illness, rather than its effects.

The fourth chakra up from the base is called the heart centre. It is located in the middle of the chest, and is responsible for our interpretations of unconditional love, self-love, openness, and trust, as well as our feelings of joy, happiness, and contentment with life. The Heart Chakra is located in the midway position of the seven chakras and links the lower chakras, which are associated with survival, creativity, birthing, and personal power, to the more spiritually expressive energy centres above. When our Heart Chakra is open and functioning fully, we embrace life. We experience an almost overwhelming sense of joy that bursts forth and positively influences every aspect of our life. A fully harmonised heart centre radiates unconditional love and in return draws the same to itself.

There is a special energy centre that is classed as the fifth chakra.

Because the heart centre is so powerful and yet so easily influenced by outside events, including the actions and words of others, and is at times quite vulnerable, it has its own guardian. There is a special energy centre that is classed as the fifth chakra. This is called the Higher Heart Chakra. It is located in between the heart and the base of the throat and is located in alignment with the thymus gland. When the higher heart centre is fully operational, we act in a compassionate manner towards others and are able to extend forgiveness and love to others and ourselves fully, without expectancy. When we genuinely act as our authentic soul self, we embrace others and ourselves with these expressions of unconditional love.

If the heart centre is the source, receiver, and reservoir for love, the higher heart centre soothes and heals the heart through compassion and forgiveness for all – including ourselves. It is a filter through which our raw emotions are passed. The higher heart centre takes on the role of minder to the heart energy. In most cases, this works as an ideal partnership. However, when we are especially excited, nervous, or angry, our feelings carry more energy and speed, which means that the filter process gets overwhelmed and only is partly effective. This is when we let words escape that we later regret!

In these circumstances, we often say things that are unnecessarily hurtful, untrue and intended to do as much damage as possible because we are responding to feeling threatened. Stress, pressure, misunderstanding, poor communication, and a history of unfaithful or broken relationships all taint our words at these times. Often, we are trying to vent our feelings and balance past wounds that have no connection with the present relationship or situation. We are acting at our most raw emotional level with little restraint.

For some, their reserves of inner self-love are so drained that they substitute the thrill of positive emotion with the adrenaline rush of finding an argument where there isn't one to be had. It is at these times for these people that the soul cries and beckons with its nudgings of guilt, embarrassment and remorse after the heat of the moment, for balance to be restored and genuine love to be fully appreciated. Much like a physical abuser may not know how to express themselves tenderly without resorting to lashing out, an emotional abuser does so because this is the example that they have most likely lived by and learned. Yet, in either case, the soul yearns for the very thing it seems to be using as its fighting tool.

How often, once you have returned to your normal, calm state, have you thought of the 'perfect' words that you wished you had said? This shows that the Higher Heart function as gatekeeper between the Heart and Throat Chakra was still working because it did not let these words escape, as they might have caused great hurt or irretrievable damage.

This partnership usually works well, allowing 'heart-felt' words to be softly filtered through the Higher Heart centre on their way to being voiced. When we are working from our Heart energy, we do not deliberately say hurtful things. Rather, we welcome closeness and have trust in the universe and ourselves. In reality, if you had spoken the 'I should have said' words, there could have been deeper hurt and more damage caused from which recovery may not have been possible. So remember that, when challenged, words are like energy arrows that can cause deep injury. Conversely, in loving circumstances, they can heal anything.

SOUL WHISPERING

There can be journeys within journeys. Watch for the signposts that can lead you much further than you could ever have imagined. Follow your passion for the right reasons. Remember that people matter more than things, and that reality does not have a replay button.

O n about the twenty-second day of pregnancy, as an igniting spark to the heart, the soul enters the foetus through what will become the nape of the neck, at the place where the forming skull meets the top of the cervical spine. At this place, there is an incredibly powerful acupuncture point that is called in traditional Chinese medicine, Fengfu, meaning 'wind hollow'.

It is here, in this small cavity, that energy gathers and forms a reservoir serving the anchoring of the soul throughout life. The soul is a form of energy; after entering the foetus at this tender hollow, it travels down the early beginnings of the spinal cord until it reaches the Higher Heart energy pool. From the Higher Heart energy centre, the soul spark moves a short distance to the physical heart where it takes up residence and ignites the heartbeat and brings the foetus to life.

So, listening to your heart rather than your head is wiser than you think, because the heart holds the awareness and whisperings of the soul and all its lifetimes of wisdom, whereas your head acts on learned behaviour, logic, and consciousness.

SOUL WHISPERING

Deep within you are the seeds that create your
roots. Cast them carefully.
Tend to them lovingly.

*T*ake a moment and place your hands in the prayer position. Notice how you naturally hold them in line with the heart. Now imagine that between your palms a chamber is created in which your truest heartfelt ambitions, wishes, desires, and prayers from your soul can be placed. Within this chamber, they become empowered. Feel the warmth and energy buzz as you focus your attention here. With your fingers pointing upwards, they act as transmitters as they point toward the universe. Breathe in and then slowly out as you imagine the energy of your thoughts rising from the space between your palms, up your fingers, and being directed to reach their destination in the heavens. Although it has been known for centuries, there is gathering scientific evidence that prayer works. Perhaps, because of the heart and soul connection, this helps explain why the potential and the results are so great.

In addition, according to Chinese medical understanding, the cells that form the heart originated from the same ones that create the small intestine. Therefore, the small intestine, or gut, and the heart are energetically linked. This is why we have a sensation known as a 'gut reaction' when we listen to our soul instincts, and equally why we experience digestive disturbances when we are stressed or upset.

Your soul's message: Aim to open your heart centres fully and live in their glory without fear, even though you may make yourself seem vulnerable. To have the strength and trust to do this takes less energy and effort than it does to keep yourself closed, withdrawn, untrusting, and alone. Love is the answer ... to any question.

Opening your heart centres brings unimaginable benefits to your life. If we could recall our early babyhood days, we'd remember nothing else but pure, unrestrained, unconditional love. For some, these days may have been overshadowed by the anxieties of new parenthood and the challenges it brings, or perhaps by the limitations of the parents' own experiences of nurturing love. Although we may be suspended by our earliest influences about how lovable we are or how deserving of love we might be, our capacity to give love depends on us as we mature.

Inevitably, as a protection strategy, we have scars incurred in the name of love that we gained through disappointments, hurts, and incidents that made us mistrust others, withdraw, or even play-out old damages whenever we encounter someone who takes a liking to us. However, if what we radiate returns to us multiplied, then we had better check the message we are putting out.

Why is awakening your heart centre so important to the soul? It is quite simple really: it allows full soul expression, which brings joy! This is the state of being that we embody when we release our self-limitations and engage in our reason for being here at this time.

Given that the soul resides in the energy of the heart and whispers caring guidance from the infinity between every heartbeat, then it follows that if the soul is to fulfill its learning for this lifetime with you as its host, it needs you to open these magnificent centres and fully experience what it is like to live as your soul intends.

To live in this way means that you are honouring your soul purpose. This is important not only because there is a predetermined contract made before you were born, but so that you as an individual can experience the pure joy of living in total harmony as your authentic self. Most people are searching for that magical something that will make their life 'click' – that elusive recipe of people, possibilities, money, and time that represents what they think it is to 'have it all'.

From your soul's point of view, it already 'has it all' and it wants to share that with you unreservedly, starting the moment you awaken yourself to the possibility. We are so often told – usually by people who think they are offering sage advice, yet who are working from their own unchallenged preprogrammed thinking – that we 'can't have it all'. My reply has always been, 'I already do!'

Living as your soul intended lets you draw more love, abundance, wealth, and support into your life than you ever imagined. You simply will not attract any negativity once you have shone the light of your soul's wisdom into every shadowy crevice of your being. When your soul has achieved its purpose through your lifetime, it will be able to ascend knowing that it has completed the next stage toward being of greater service to all humanity because it has gained further understanding about being human. Connecting with your heart energy allows this to happen.

SOUL WHISPERING

As our soul rests in the heart, when we connect
with nature, and feel the joy swell within us, we
awaken the memory and connection to
the source.

The Heart Chakra, which sits in the centre of the chest, is closely linked to the health of the physical heart. Classically, when we loose the joy from our life, our heart starts to run on empty. Then, when we need it most or have managed to make some significant changes that should allow our heart, and the heart centres, the opportunity to properly serve us, there is nothing there to draw upon. Tragically, in these cases, it is the physical heart that suffers most. It is all too easy to live and plan for tomorrow, and yet your heart energy knows only today. If we 'lose heart' in our work, relationships, or if our ambitions seem impossible to fulfill, the heart energy will drain rapidly. To remedy this, note how many times in a day you forecast achieving your happiness at some point in the future. How many times do you say or think, 'Everything will be okay when' or 'I can't wait until … and then everything will be just how I want it to be'. There is no value in working for retirement; there is only value in working for today. Watch the clock and it moves slowly; engross yourself in your present interests and time moves with you. Being in the present moment keeps your energy where it should be and ensures that it will be there for every tomorrow, no matter what you decide to do with it.

In almost every return to the soul school called Earth, one of the foundational experiential cornerstones is to be loved and extend love. Why is love so important to the growth of the soul? Is it because our soul is never satisfied and is always looking for something better? Is it addicted through some powerful memory to the initial feelings of first falling in love? Or is it the chance to fall in love one or more times during a lifetime, perhaps as compensation for the trials the soul will face during its many lives?

The answer to these questions is that love is the most powerful force of all. Without it, chaos can arise in our behaviour. The soul needs to anchor this essential emotion within its host so it has a firm foundation from which to operate. When we are open to embracing true unconditional love, we experience the most amazing feelings of joy and happiness. This is what makes your soul sing. We feel totally alive and free. Nothing is wrong or out of balance in our world. If we lived in an ideal world, we would all support each other, as we blissfully existed at this level permanently. The sad truth is that life and its reality all too quickly shut down our willing hearts. Because we encounter people, partners, and even parents whose souls are at different levels of evolution than our own, we find ourselves amidst experiences that can be damaging and make us recoil, thus slowing our soul's progress.

If our heart centre is subdued or even closed, we may remove ourselves emotionally from the company of others and avoid forming close relationships for fear of being hurt. This may be a natural behaviour to engage in for a time after suffering a blow to the heart, and in some ways it is quite curative. However, it is not a healthy way to continually exist. If we do, we suffer from loneliness, isolation, and a lack of trust, and find ourselves becoming judgmental, critical, and resentful of others. This can lead to feelings of superiority if we consider others inferior as a defense mechanism, and yet this is just a subconscious way of distracting our inner knowledge from admitting the truth that, deep down, we feel inferior. The saddest part of living with a closed heart centre is that we are unable to reach out to others in unconditional love, and this means that we cannot accept it either.

Usually if the heart centre is not fully functioning, the higher heart centre will be closed also. If this area is not functioning properly, we may act harshly, showing a lack of compassion, and we may be unable to love others or ourselves fully, without criticism or judgment. Further, because we are not accepting of others and ourselves, we cannot extend forgiveness. If the higher heart centre were out of balance and malfunctioning, it would be like a hard, rough-surfaced fruit that has been allowed to dry out naturally. How can any juicy energy meant to soothe the heart's emotional wounds and nurture love for ourselves and others possibly flow into or out of it?

Awakening your heart centres can happen at any time. Because of the wealth of unconditional love and forgiveness that naturally begins to flow, any feelings of regret, remorse, guilt, or self-recrimination are assuaged and replaced with only genuinely positive emotions. If the attempt to unite with the love, forgiveness, and compassion of the heart centres is not genuine, the old behaviour will quickly return.

One of the most powerful ways of starting to open your heart centres is to adopt a daily practice of self-honouring. This is simple, and can lead to many other positive transformations in your life because it is intended to bring to you all the benefits of having healthy, open, and balanced heart centres.

SOUL WHISPERING

To know yourself is to know your soul.

*I*n the comfort of your first waking moments each morning, say the following either silently or aloud: 'I start this day with love in my heart'. Repeat this several times. Next, as you make your way to the bathroom, say: 'With every step, I leave a trail of love and light'. And as you go about your day, make your mantra, 'I am light filled, loving, and wise'. If you are challenged or temporarily knocked out of your thinking regarding a decision, ask yourself, 'What would my loving, joy-filled soul do in this circumstance?' Listen to the words of wisdom or 'coincidences' that bring answers and you will never act against your highest good.

Some people find it nurturing and healing, as well as a good reminder to always work from their heart centres, to wear the colours associated with each. For the Heart Chakra the colour is green – a vibrant mid tone that reflects nature. The Higher Heart Chakra resonates with the colour pink. Interestingly, a study some years ago revealed that the most popular, pleasing flowers were those with luscious green foliage and beautiful, soft-pink blossoms. Often, if we observe fashion, the trends reflect what we need as a society. Over the recent few years, I have observed a constant presence of green and pink colours either mixed in one garment or sold as complementary separates.

So often in today's lifestyle, we are challenged by the very emotion that is intended to bring ultimate joy and happiness. Awakening and connecting with your heart centres is not just about love and learning to give and receive it healthily. It is this and so much more.

To nurture your heart centres, practice random acts of kindness. Smile at a stranger. Most people will smile back, and hopefully they will, in turn, smile at others. Extend a helping hand without concern for reciprocation. The users and takers will quickly reveal themselves. However, the good you give out will return to you 100 fold. Never be afraid to take a deep breath and let your heart centres glow like the sun. You can encourage this by thinking to yourself as you breathe in, 'I am joy. I am my soul. I am love!' Try it. You have everything to gain.

CHAPTER 4

Your Soul Speaks Through Your Health

CHAPTER 4

Your Soul Speaks Through Your Health

*When you need to know where your life needs healing,
look at your health.*

*M*y initial clients who sought treatment when I started my life as a therapist needed physical help with muscular and skeletal problems. Using the training I had received from some of the leading pioneers in Complementary Medicine – all now recognised as authoritative, world-class teachers – I responded enthusiastically and these clients received the benefit. As my skills and experience grew, so too did the complexity of the treatment requests. This reinforced the concept that one is only taken to the limit of their ability when they are ready.

Over time, as my learning and studies took me further into the realms of energy medicine, I came to understand the origins of disease and view the conditions being presented to me with completely different eyes.

SOUL WHISPERING

*Take heed. I, your soul, speak of disharmony
in many ways.*

*T*ake a look at the symbolic character of an ailment; is there congestion, stagnation, swelling, degeneration, or distortion? Every condition reflects an emotional quality that has an influential effect through the mind on the body. It is widely accepted now that what we think about we bring about, and in relation to health this is no different.

What must be emphasised is that, when exploring the source of a condition – given that most are derived from our behaviour, emotions, or thoughts – it may seem natural to feel guilty and blame ourselves. However, these two unbeneficial emotional burdens have no place in the recovery process. Getting stuck in the mire of culpability only consumes valuable energy otherwise needed for healing. It goes right along with the message that every minute spent stressing and feeling low is a minute of lost happiness. If we view illness as a reflection of our journey to date and treat it as a call to action, we can start to reveal one of the greatest strengths of the soul – its ability to guide from within and provide us with an opportunity to improve our lives.

SOUL WHISPERING

*When energy accumulates and stagnates,
the natural flow of life ceases and challenge
steps in.*

$\mathcal{I}$t is through the emotions that the soul communicates, because this is part of the language of the soul. We all have a history of events, emotional behaviours, beliefs, and values that help us navigate our experiences and negotiate our way through each day. Life can certainly present some challenging circumstances, and yet some people thrive while others wither as a result. What determines the degree to which our mental, physical, or emotional health will be influenced, is how we choose to respond to a situation or circumstance.

Remember that your soul is here to learn and therefore life is not going to be all smooth and rosy. In some cases, it is going to be tremendously challenging and difficult. One of the secrets to successful soul growth also yields greater emotional strength. This nugget of wisdom is simple: View the events in your life from the perspective of what you can learn from them. Set aside the instinct to look at events from a human-cost mindset as much as you can without becoming cold and emotionless, and try to look at them from a soul growth viewpoint and then absorb the lesson. Incorporate it into your everyday life, and since you have paid attention, you will not have to learn the same things again. Here is where you may need the guidance of a soul coach or mentor. This is an investment that will reap its rewards for the rest of your life and will enhance your soul's journey.

Keeping the emotional and psychological welfare of my client in mind, when I work with individuals who have been able to step out of the way of the intensely personal impact and reframe it around what they can positively draw from it, I have seen healing miracles happen before my eyes. By dealing with situations in this way, we are able to move forward in life, enriched by understanding the experience or challenge, and make a full recovery much quicker.

SOUL WHISPERING

*Honouring the journey of a soul means forgiving
ourselves for our humanness.*

*I*t is when we internalise and personalise the emotional value of events that our health, character, and life begins to be negatively influenced and defined. When we give these events or the people who instigated them power and control, allowing ourselves to build upon them by continually thinking about the hurt, the anger, the injustice, or our victimisation that we become stuck in that space, and the energy stops flowing. If we could employ soul consciousness, we would freely view life's events as the opportunities for growth they are intended to be.

This does not mean that we need become harsh or uncaring, or that we are not affected by personal tragedy. What it does mean is that connecting with the underlying meaning from a greater soul perspective can help ease the pain and nurture the healing process.

The bottom line here is that we have a choice about how we respond to events and challenges. We can choose to become a victim, remaining incarcerated in a cell of our own making, or we can choose to springboard ourselves beyond the initial trauma and become richer for it. The choice is ultimately ours.

When you choose to learn from a situation and release yourself from patterns of negativity, hurt, anger, guilt, fear, or any other self-limiting mindset that you have been harbouring, your soul rejoices and supports the next stage of your journey. Bringing this concept to bear on your health requires a closer look at the language of illness. This reflects part of the concept of soulistic empowerment discussed in Chapter 12.

There are three main ways that the soul talks to us through our health. The first is through the condition of the skeleton. The second is the condition of the body's main organs, which is covered in chapter 5 titled 'The Soul Doctor'. The third – the focus in this chapter – is through the hormone producing and secreting glands of the endocrine system. For some, taking an organic approach may be more comfortable, while for others, understanding the language of the hormones as they act as spokespersons for their corresponding chakras is more interesting. Either way, the soul speaks with integrity and appreciates your attention.

Here, we are going to explore what our eyes cannot perceive – the hormones and their emotional, energetic influence. Everything is energy, and all things, living or not, exists at a certain rate of vibration. A rock, a butterfly, a tree, a table, a voice singing a melody, or a child are all made up of energy vibrating at its own specific rate, which is what determines its density. Some things vibrate incredibly quickly, such as a thought or emotion, and therefore do not have a physical form, while others operate at a much slower rate of vibration, and therefore become dense and take on a tangible shape, such as a human being. The faster the vibration, the less shape something has, to the point where it is invisible to our naked eye, yet it still exists. The slower the vibration means the harder the object. Even though a rock vibrates very slowly, it still vibrates at a certain frequency.

Emotions carry an energetic 'weight' and value. We can witness their effects as evidence of their existence, yet we cannot physically see an emotion. Have you ever entered an empty room and felt the remnants of an argument that recently took place there? Or when viewing a potential new home, have you sensed if it is a happy, welcoming place? These are examples of emotional energy.

There is energy all around us, continually washing over us and running through us. However, most of us cannot see these different levels of vibration because our earthly eyes cannot see beyond certain frequencies of light, which limits our perception to a refined colour spectrum. Some people, however, maintain their ability to operate at a higher frequency and can see auras, light beings, spirits, and other such energies. We can all become reacquainted with these natural talents with the right training. Because we are beings of light, we operate at a certain vibration. Our soul also has a frequency that allows it to become slower and manifest as a physical form and then release itself when its host can no longer support and anchor its energy.

When a soul is in residence, it radiates an aura around its host. An aura is a multi-layered energy cocoon that acts as both a filter and protective barrier to shield us from the rawness of the world around us. The soul maintains a connection with the outside world through its sentinels, otherwise known as the body's seven main chakras, which act like portals through this shield.

We pick up on what others are thinking through our aura, and then these thoughts are filtered as they move inward toward the chakras, where, ultimately, they may have a physical effect.

Equally, what we think and hold strongly in our minds can be sent out beyond our physical shell, via the chakra vortices, to rest in our aura. This is what others sense when we are in a strong state of emotion. If you stand near someone who is angry, newly in love, sad, or carrying any other strong emotion, you will sense it in your aura first, and then your mind will translate it so that you can put it into words. So, the emotions and thoughts around us can be pulled into our very core by the chakras.

Do you know the language of the chakras? As mentioned before, chakra is Sanskrit for 'wheel' – a spinning circle of energy that receives, assimilates, translates, and expresses the energy of the universal life force. There are known to be hundreds of minor chakras found in the auric layers. However, the five main chakras located along the spine and the additional two in the head are the most commonly referred to. Each is inextricably linked to one of the main hormone-producing glands. They are essentially vacuums for bringing the external world deep inside your physical self. Your health is a reflection of your thinking; you are what you think because your body takes you quite literally.

The universe of energy is mostly unseen. However, it is through our emotions that life gets its measure. Some emotions are fleeting, although many, when held long enough and strong enough, become denser and develop into significantly bulky energetic baggage. Left unchecked – yet often being fuelled continually – the level of vibration of these emotions slows even further, and their impact within the organs and tissues of the body starts to manifest. These emotions, then, become a presence – a blockage, a tumour, or a disease that reveals one's true inner emotional health, views, and responses to life's events.

Even if you remove the tumour, have the skilful surgeons found the core reason for its growth? The energetic seeds of anger, grief, low self-esteem, fear, worry, hurt, bitterness, lack of self-love or even self-hatred, will never show up in a blood test, grow in a laboratory dish, or turn blue with a known chemical catalyst. Energy exists everywhere – within and without the body. It does not conform to explorations by chemicals and cannot be cut out. It simply is.

So what does your illness mean? It conveys the message that you would benefit from exploring your emotional energy, your life path, and your soul journey. Where and how you manifest your disease, condition or illness may be a calling from your soul to your specific area of need. In relation to your chakras, each one represents a key emotion and basic need. Our emotions may arise from events caused by others around us, or they may be of our own making, within our own minds. These emotions can be a mixture of both positive and less-desirable forces. When a chakra responds to our inner choir, it transfers this impulse to its associated hormonal gland. In turn, the gland responds by producing its secretions, which are then distributed via the blood stream to its target organ. This is one way in which an emotion can have a contributory effect on your physical health.

The examples of this are all around, in the people you see who are ill, who express themselves through the imbalances in their health and approach to life. Many people adopt a personal lifestyle like that of perpetually running on a 'hamster wheel' that calls for your attention, but this hamster wheel, although it is round and may be coloured gold, is not a halo turned on its side! Every illness is an example. You can gain many insights by looking at where your health problems focus themselves.

You can gain many insights by looking at where your health problems focus themselves.

Once the energy of external events is filtered through the layers of the aura, it is drawn to one of the seven main chakras by being funneled down the chakra vortex into the chakra proper. From there, the energy starts to condense and therefore affect the organ or gland concerned. The chakras can help us connect with the universe and ourselves. Each has its own specialized functions. When the chakric system is balanced, the body feels unified and in harmony. However, the chakras can become chocked and stagnated through stress, emotional discord, illness, medication, childhood trauma, belief systems, hating one's job, and many other typical life experiences. We develop coping strategies that actually serve to maintain the blockage rather than look to its cause and work to dissolve and resolve this. This is why taking a look at the fundamental influences of each of the main chakras can help you gather insights that will help you progress toward a better state of health.

SOUL WHISPERING

We are only as strong as our foundations.

The first of the chakras – the Base or Root Chakra – is located at the tailbone. This spinning vortex is aligned with the adrenal glands, which help us in situations where 'fight or flight' is required. The energy of the Base Chakra is concerned with survival.

When we are born, our Base Chakra remains connected to our mother's for a short while, and it takes about twelve weeks for us to realise that we are separate from her. During this time, we are highly aware of this connection. Because our energetic link will close, this is a crucial time for the mother-child bonding process to be established. The key qualities for this chakra focus on having solid foundations in life, protection, and survival. This allows us to make our own place in life and literally put down roots. In order to successfully achieve this, it's important that our needs are met.

When one's Base Chakra is blocked or shut down, one will often display emotions such as anger, greed, lust, jealousy, excessive drive and ambition, and fear. Further, when the Base Chakra is blocked or out of balance, we may well manifest physical symptoms in the kidneys, bladder, rectum, hips, and spine. Because this chakra deals with our foundations, it is also associated with our tribal relationships and cohesiveness.

From a spiritual perspective, this chakra is concerned with self-awareness. When we think of having a stable core upon which we build our life, this is where the Root or Base Chakra holds its strength for us. This includes feeling secure in our relationships, career, home, finances, and bodily health. Back problems – especially in the lower spine – speak of a need to re-establish or strengthen one's foundation and support network in life. I have treated many clients who suddenly developed back pain that coincided with a loss of support from someone close. The spine serves as a pillar from which everything else extends. Think of where you draw support from, and explore whether those relationships or arrangements are solid. Consider the direction of your career, your home or living conditions, your financial security, and most importantly the quality of your relationships with the people whom you consider integral to your life and future.

To strengthen the Base Chakra, use this affirmation: I am my own pillar of strength, and yet I have abundant support around me at all times. The universe supports me.

SOUL WHISPERING

When you exercise your creativity, your soul
rejoices in celebration.

*T*he next chakra we encounter as we move up the spine is the Sacral Chakra, located just below the navel. This chakra is aligned with the lower large intestine and the reproductive organs, which are associated with the sex hormones. It speaks of creativity, birthing new ideas and projects, which are a gift and an expression of the condition of the soul. We all have a need to create and metaphorically give birth to something expressive and intrinsic to ourselves – our offering to the world.

79

In spiritual terms, this chakra houses the attribute of self-respect. However, it can vary between demonstrating unconditional love and possessiveness, so it is, therefore, associated with interpersonal relationships. To keep this chakra strong and free flowing, we need to maintain creativity within our close relationships and nurture a healthy sexual desire.

Creativity is truly the key to allowing energy to flow to and through this chakra. Use it in everything you do, and your world will become simply magical beyond your wildest dreams. From mundane tasks to adventurous challenges to routine daily events, infuse your world with creative living and you will transform yourself and quite possibly those around you.

When creativity is suppressed and emotional pain associated with relationships is not resolved and dissolved, the related organs begin to malfunction. Problems in the sacral region, including the reproductive organs, could indicate difficult relationships with a partner, one's self, or others in general.

The soul has no gender. Therefore, it is the personality that takes on a gender. Through our Sacral Chakra, we express this aspect of our individuality as we present ourselves to the world.

To balance and harmonise the Sacral Chakra, use this affirmation: I honour and give birth to myself as I release the pain of all past relationships and injuries, as an act of unconditional love for myself.

SOUL WHISPERING

*All that you are and all that you can be is
delivered through your soul.*

*T*he third of the lower chakras is known as the Solar Plexus. As energy rises from the Sacral and Base Chakras, it passes to this chakra, which is the seat of personal power and the chamber of self-worth, self-respect, and self-esteem, as well as their counterparts, self-loathing, hatred of self and others, and self-denial. Sitting at the base of the sternum in the centre where the two sides of the rib cage create an apex, this chakra's associated organs are the liver, spleen, stomach, and small intestine.

It is here at this point that healing energy is channeled through its correlated gland, the pancreas, in association with its endocrine functions of dealing with the sweet foods we eat. The connection between the universe and body is strongest here, and this chakra serves as a union for the ethereal and physical planes.

The range of emotions represented in this extremely powerful chakra extends from anger and rejection to unworthiness, lack of willpower, and mentally rigidity, leading to a character who thinks it is always right! With this scope of emotional expression possible, it is essential that this chakra be in harmony and well maintained, if we are to lead a balanced emotional life.

The Solar Plexus Chakra is concerned with one's relationship with one's self. We hide our true self here, and use this energy chamber as the place where we make our own rules about life, its direction, and how we will operate in relationships. The Solar Plexus is the place of the birth of the ego. When we operate from an unbalanced Solar Plexus Chakra, we bully our way around people, seeing our own needs as the most important.

Part of what forms this persona is the fact that the Solar Plexus takes on the opinions of others and doesn't let them go. Evidence of this can be seen in conditions such as stomach disorders, diabetes, chronic fatigue syndrome, low immunity, and blood pressure irregularities.

So many people are blocked at the level of the Solar Plexus Chakra, and so hold themselves in a perpetual state of being unfulfilled. The soul may reside in the Heart Chakra above, but it is within the Solar Plexus Chakra that unconditional love begins. So many people guard themselves from fully engaging with others by either physically or mentally crossing their arms in a protective manner across their chest, effectively blocking their Solar Plexus energy. If we feel threatened, or if we do not want to 'connect' with someone, this is a good mechanism to employ. However, if we are in the habit of maintaining a protective or defensive stance, we are unwittingly blocking our energy flow.

It is through our Solar Plexus that we radiate our perceived place in the world. When we are in balance and harmony, others receive this as a gentle, welcoming energy that is comfortable to be around. Out of balance, it can be repelling and arrogant.

To harmonise the Solar Plexus Chakra, use the affirmation: I am in balance with my physical and emotional self. I radiate warmth and withhold judgment, criticism, and expectancy in all my relationships, especially with myself.

SOUL WHISPERING

When faced with a challenge, ask yourself, 'If I act out of "love", what would I do in this circumstance?' Your soul will answer through your heart.

*T*he Heart Chakra is the centre of the most important emotions, love and joy. This meaningful chakra is often described in conjunction with its guardian, the Higher Heart Chakra. The Heart

Chakra's related endocrine gland is the thymus, located in the centre of the chest, which it shares with the Higher Heart Chakra.

Naturally, the emotional character of the Heart Chakra is self-love. This is possibly the most difficult and most often denied emotion we carry within ourselves. So often in our early life, we are told to always put others' needs before our own, and that to honour oneself with loving kindness is a self-indulgent act that is to be frowned upon. And yet, if we cannot actively and genuinely love ourselves, warts and all, how can we possibly hope to truly give and appreciate love in any relationship?

When embodied souls forsake themselves and are hijacked by the spirit and personality, they lose their joy in the pursuit of more money and material gain. Guilt then invades their joy, and hurt becomes the blood that courses through the vessels. The higher wisdom of the soul knows that these people had everything they sought within them all the time. They could already attract all of the most valuable commodities in life, but they thought that by surrounding themselves with the shiniest baubles and bangles that the better things would come. These things, however, do not make the heart and soul sing.

All these people will ever get is a reflection of their external measure; something that glitters always seeks a mirror to observe its reflection, but just like its appearance in the mirror, it is only real when the reflection is present. Would it not be better to reflect the inner radiance of one's soul light out into the world and receive that back? This is a reflection that reveals inner truth, wisdom, self-love, and strong core values. It will also reflect one's wounds and self-sabotage, so that one can be healed and the soul can progress.

The heart's energy is focused on being able to give and take unconditionally. The Heart Chakra is so potent that it sends out its vibrations for thirty feet in every direction. This is why one can feel the emotion of love or attraction across a room! Remember, though, that the heart can also radiate hurt and guilt, and this is equally detectable.

When the joy is leached from life, the heart energy struggles to meet the demands of the rest of the physical body. Happiness, which is the constant quest of us all – despite being, perhaps, to some people a naive and childish word – is the secret of longevity. And if it is a childish word, why is it wrong to embrace life with a youthful heart and the delight of innocent wonder?

Maintain your heart energy by becoming comfortable with the concept of self-love, and use this as your measure of how to respond when difficult decisions are to be made. You will never create regret if you are able to follow this guidance.

An affirmation to heal and strengthen the Heart Chakra: 'I am self-love. I rejoice in its freedom and wealth every day of my life'.

SOUL WHISPERING

Silence is the master of the soul and the mystery of the mind.

*A*cting as spokesperson for the Heart Chakras is the Throat Chakra – the communication centre – that rests in the base of the neck, in line with the thyroid gland. The hormones produced by this gland control the body's metabolism. One could draw parallels between metabolism and one's openness and ability to communicate. The Throat Chakra is the seat of communication in all its forms – verbal and non-verbal, listening and being heard.

With the wide variety of vocal potential available to each of us, it is hardly surprising that this chakra is associated with self-expression. When we feel restricted in our freedom, we are prone to manifest conditions that reflect in the lungs, throat, and thyroid. Our health and quality of life is the sum total of our individual emotions and experiences. Why is it common to stifle one's true self behind words of expectation and criticism, when with each utterance the soul cringes in its own disbelief? Listen to your heart. Listen as it begs to be heard. Speak words of encouragement, love, and support, and you will receive the same in return. Honour others by engaging their messages. Don't let yourself or anyone else become stifled, as it will only harm you both.

The Throat Chakra beckons for space and choice. You can honour this basic need by being in nature, singing like no one is listening, and allowing yourself to voice what your soul guides you to through your feelings and visions.

To strengthen your Throat Chakra, affirm: I communicate clearly. I listen to others with my full attention, and I am listened to in return. As I seek to understand others, I will be understood.

SOUL WHISPERING

I bring wisdom and knowledge. Let yourself benefit from my wisdom. Your life will be richer when you listen to the voice within.

*T*he innate anchor point for inner knowledge is the Third Eye, or Brow Chakra. Located in the centre point between the eyebrows, it is directly in line with the pineal and pituitary glands deep within the brain. This powerful energy-collecting point amplifies your psychic or deeply intuitive abilities. Physically, it influences and coordinates the balance of hormones, which ultimately controls the normal functions within the whole body.

It could be said that if the Third Eye Chakra is out of balance, so are the hormones. Think of how many women you know who are 'hormonally challenged', and at the same time are shut off from their intuitive gifts! I also see this effect represented through conditions in the surrounding facial areas, such as blocked sinuses, headaches, and eye problems. These conditions are all characterised by congestion and feeling 'stuck' in one's present circumstances.

When the Third Eye Chakra is blocked, closed, or out of balance, we will often find ourselves feeling confused about our roles and how to move forward when we seek to bring understanding to our life. The energy of the Third Eye needs vision and balance to help it function best for our benefit. This can be achieved by taking time for one's self, to meditate and view challenge as an opportunity for growth, in the sure and certain knowledge that life's situations and circumstances are perpetually in a state of change.

To unblock the Third Eye Chakra, affirm regularly: I clearly see the positive aspects in my life. I have the freedom to explore and live by my inner truth.

SOUL WHISPERING

When seeking peace and connection with the divine, look to the heavens through your heart.

*F*inally, although there are many other chakras worth considering, the seventh main chakra of the bodily system is the Crown Chakra which sits directly above the pituitary gland. It is so powerful that it acts as a beacon, radiating a beam of luminescent brilliance toward the soul plane in the heavens.

The seat of self-knowledge, this powerful chakra acts as an anchor for the constant feed of wisdom and support readily available to each and every one of us from the infinite wealth of the universe. It is also the source of the tunnel of light so often spoken of in reports, after recovery, of the events and visions in the moments after death. This is the portal through which the exiting soul bids farewell to its most recent host as it starts its journey Home.

So many people suffer with tired, over-burdened brains, which lead to headaches, migraines, foggy thinking, and even tumours. This is possibly because the gateway to the universal source of energy flow is blocked or sealed shut. This causes the energy rising from the earth up through the lower chakras like a powerful fountain to become trapped, stagnant, and congested, gnawing at the energy transmitter in the brain. If this energy highway is so important, how does it become blocked?

A baby is born with more knowledge than is can express. The fontanels – the gaps between the plates of the skull – are still open, and there is one directly above the Crown Chakra as already discussed. It is through this opening that the connection with the universal source is maintained in early life. As the child grows, the skull naturally forms a fully protective enclosure, yet the energy opening and the connection remain.

When the child becomes mobile, and especially when it starts to express itself, it immediately begins to be governed and guided to the best ability of its parents. Many children speak of memories of past lives and talk to 'invisible' friends, which is a sign of their openness and soul memory. However, since a child learns what it lives, before it can question what it is taught, the hard-wiring of the individual is often affected by beliefs and views not its own. The attributes that are not determined by the home environment are cemented when the youngster enters formal schooling, where individualism is homogenized to ensure that learning markers and curricular goals are reached. Unfortunately, this is often at the expense of the voice of the soul, which learns to either be obedient or be an outcast.

It is from these early stages of development that our Crown Chakra starts to suffer its blockages. As we progressively loose our connection with the universe, so too do we become more trapped in our earth-bound reality, which is when our health starts to reflect what is happening in our lives. The Crown Chakra yearns for peace, yet often finds itself wallowing in despair. In order to free our energy and re-establish our connection with the universe, we need to concentrate on nurturing an acceptance of ourselves as physical and spiritual beings uniting for the benefit of both.

The Crown Chakra responds to this affirmation: I open myself to my divine connection. Energy flows freely to me, through me, and from me, energizing and harmonizing me continually.

Having considered the existence of these amazingly influential energy centres, perhaps you can gain some insight into some of the seemingly small annoyances you have experienced in your health. Working with the chakra energy awareness is a deeper level of understanding, and yet it also utilises 'e–motion' – energy in motion.

Everything in this life begins with a thought; this is the spark of the creative process, and life is all about creation. It doesn't matter if you are writing a letter, creating a nice home for yourself or those you love, or building a global corporate structure – it all begins with a thought. We can see the external evidence of this at work, so it is only natural that we can look within ourselves and see the same forces of creation.

If you understand your chakra energy and the thoughts, needs, and beliefs that influence its healthy flow or stagnation, it takes only a few minutes of focused intention in daily practice to start to unravel that which may have become tangled and twisted. I have used affirmations for over two decades, and they work. There is no question. I use them with clients, and often, when deep healing is needed. Through the practitioner. When I work with ThetaDNA Healing, a type of affirmation is used to check my clients core beliefs on several levels. A core belief is something that, whether true or not, they believe is real for them. Once discovered, if these beliefs are negatively influencing their life, they can be altered and replaced with ones that are more positive and nurturing.

Take a few minutes to regularly repeat the affirmations as given – or create your own – and you will start to feel and see the differences very quickly. To work with the whole chakra system, it is possible to use a single affirmation.

A unifying and balancing affirmation for your chakra system is: I am a bridge of light from the earth to the universe; my energy flows freely and nourishes me in every way.

Remember, if a thought can create anything, you are in the most powerful place in your life in this moment!

CHAPTER 5

The Soul Doctor

CHAPTER 5

The Soul Doctor

Emotions are the energy of life, the creator of oneself,
and the healer of the soul.

Long before the popular concept of mind-body medicine and metaphysics took hold in the West, the ancient Orientals understood illness based on the energy each main body organ represented and housed. When an 'e-motion', literally energy in motion, becomes too influential, the organ begins to suffer and illness starts to surface. Resolve the underpinning emotion and dismantle the mindset that held it in place, and the ailment will start to dissolve! This sounds easy, I know, but recovery only takes a willingness to begin this process.

Keep in mind that it is how we choose to deal with these emotions that determines the quality of our soulistic health – in other words, the health of the soul charged by the emotions, represented through the health of the individual.

SOUL WHISPERING

Free yourself in one act of grace – Forgive.

$\mathcal{W}$e all know it to be true, though we often put it to the back of our minds, that our health is our greatest asset. So often, it is not until we experience a major scare that we move this vital component of our life up the rankings of importance and take note.

It is fair to say that good, reliable health is created through a number of factors. However, given that statistics indicate that we are all prone to develop a major illness, such as cancer, at least six times during our lifetime, why do some fall victim to this most common disease and others do not?

Health is not just the lack of illness. Nor is it measured merely by physical fitness and endurance. It is the presence of abundant vitality, shimmering wellness, emotional balance, beauty radiating from within without relying on pearlescent genetics, resilient happiness, and the ability to deal with external pressures in a way that does not allow them internal squatting space.

Have you ever met someone who simply oozes magnificent health? I have. On getting to know them better, what they possess may not be good genes or the ability to afford a personal trainer or top quality mega vitamins.

THEIR SECRET IS IN THEIR APPROACH TO LIFE FROM THE INSIDE OUT!

*T*his is their elixir that fuels the fountain of youth. Imagine a life where each morning when you wake up, you feel exhilarated and welcome the start of a new day, even if it is the depths of winter and the weather is miserable! Consider gliding through your day, handling the occasional stresses and challenges with efficient detachment and dissolving the unexpected ones with ease. Daydream a scene where you are facing deadlines and pressures from your line manager and you embrace the opportunity as one in which you can turn it to your advantage to show how you can creatively and resourcefully manage yourself, and perhaps others, for the best possible outcome.

Fantastic! So, how is this possible? To begin with, it is important to recognise one major thing. Radiant health and well-being cannot be bought! Yes, good general health can be polished through exercise, proper diet, and good grooming, however, the final finish is only as good as the foundation onto which the trimmings are applied.

SOUL WHISPERING

Your outer reality reflects your choices; your health reflects your inner reality.

*T*o nurture amazing health, we need to start from within. To do this, we must initially look at what makes good health in the first place. Intrinsically, the type of health we all seek to possess is made up of a balance of reliable physical capability, a strong, balanced mental platform, and a rainbow of emotions that collectively create a whole person capable of appropriately responding to life and its challenges. In addition, having a comfortable and personal spiritual connection and centeredness that anchors us to our inner truth helps guide our decisions, which are then reflected to the outer world.

From these foundational pillars, we can build a true sense of wellness and meet any challenge, of any magnitude, on any given day. We see this in others who effortlessly deal with and overcome stressful work situations. For some, their challenge is to survive their domestic environment. Then again, an alarming number of innocent people must make the best of their present circumstances, over which they often have no control.

I am sure that you have had experiences when you were not feeling 100 per cent physically, though your inner attitude was 1000 per cent, and you received comments about how wonderful you looked. The secret to this outer radiance is your well-spring of inner strength.

Your soul wants you to understand that in order to generate endless magnificent health, you need to tap into the depths of your true self and allow a steady stream of this light to shine through your eyes, your smile, and most importantly your heart.

When you can sustain this mode of being, you will enjoy what many can barely conceive of. You will not only positively influence everyone you meet, but you will start a subtle series of changes in those with whom you spend the most time. One of two things will happen: either your nearest and dearest will gather closer and subconsciously begin to mimic your ways, hoping to tap into your secret well-spring without actually doing their own foundational work to generate their unique radiance, or they will not be able to understand or sit comfortably in your presence, and they will keep their distance while observing you closely. Either way, you have helped them understand a bit more about where they are in their own soul evolution, whether they consciously realise it or not.

When the soul is in tune with the life it is meant to live, vibrant health is the natural and only outcome. Why? Because when the soul is in harmony with its host, the affects of disharmony and disease do not have an opportunity to manifest.

There are many public figures – in politics, business, the media, and in our own world – who do a magnificent job fulfilling their chosen role in whatever capacity that may be. However, if we were to look at their track record of health issues, the stark truth may reveal that although they believe they are following a path to which they feel drawn, perhaps it has changed, though they are not able to jump off their self-made hamster wheel.

SOUL WHISPERING

Vibrant health is a reflection of one's energetic frequency.

*W*hen your inner equilibrium is overburdened or unable to find its own natural balance, you are susceptible to a host of minor complaints. To most of us, these are annoying niggles that may or may not warrant a trip to your doctor. Generally, we just battle on, ignoring the persistent knocking at the door of our common sense, wisdom, and inner knowing. The practice of reflective health awareness is informative, because it is highly specific when things are not as they should be. There is a huge body of knowledge available today that focuses on metaphysics or the mind-body connection for whole health. There is even a branch of science, called psychoneuroimmunology (PNI for short), that has proven that the cells of the body 'talk' to each other through chemicals called neurotransmitters.

What does this mean? In short, your body responds to every thought, belief, and emotion that passes through it, and it forms part of your personality, belief system, and consciousness. While this may indicate that your cells are in a permanently chaotic state of confusion and congestion, the body has learned to distinguish the meaningful triggers from the minor ones. An even greater effect is attributed to the memories, thoughts, issues, and emotional dealings that have long since been relegated to the subconscious.

Your soul speaks through your health. So, if we want to take advantage of our full health potential, we must learn the language of our body and respond accordingly. In general, the health of your skeleton reflects your attitudes, and the health of your organs reflects your emotions and beliefs about yourself and the world around you (whether they have a truthful foundation or not). The energy load of your emotions and beliefs governs your health. Therefore, your state of well-being is intrinsically associated with your soul.

Your soul's message: Illness, of the mind, body, or spirit shows us where our life is out of balance. There are messages within each state of health. A wise person explores, listens, is honest with himself, and is brave enough to make changes when they are necessary.

The ancient cultures knew this truth, and it is increasingly becoming familiar knowledge in the West through the growing numbers of therapists, healers, yoga classes, meditation meetings, and available information highlighting how your body speaks your mind. The language is simple to learn and can be applied instantly. It is all about parallels. This is about looking at the role of a certain part of the body when it is functioning correctly, and then looking at what it means when that part ceases to operate properly.

For each and every ailment, we can start to affect a remedy through the healing power of affirmations. These are positive statements, spoken or written in the present tense, that focus on your aims, desires, ambitions, and goals as though they are already a reality. An example of an affirmation to help address prolonged ill health would be: 'Every day, in every way, I am getting healthier and stronger'. The use of affirmations was made popular in modern times by leading inspirational gurus such as Louise L. Hay (who healed herself of cancer) and Dr. Wayne Dwyer, among others.

I first came across this concept in 1990, when I attended a workshop presented by Dr. Christine Page titled, 'The Messages of Disease'. The day was fascinating and filled my head with numerous answers regarding the clients and patients I was treating at the time. This new and somewhat mystical way of understanding illness ignited a spark within me that has continued to direct my personal and professional relationships. In 1995, I become aware of the expanded concepts of the mind-body connection through the writing of Louise L. Hay, who wrote in detail of every emotion and thought fuelling a representation in the body. In 1997, I became a qualified Louise L. Hay, You Can Heal Your Life, accredited teacher. Since that intensive personal development course, my life has changed and I have been empowered in every dimension beyond all recognition. I have personally experienced the power of these affirmations at work, and I have literally used this simple healing force in thousands of sessions with my clients over the intervening years. It may seem too easy. However, when you employ the law of attraction through powerful affirmations for personal healing and health, miracles start to happen, and you will attract that which is meant for you, if it is in your highest good.

SOUL WHISPERING

The universe is waiting to share its power and wisdom with you. Just ask, and if it is in your best interest for growth and development, you will receive.

*T*here are literally dozens of ways to create an affirmation to help with a particular aspect of health. Creating your own is always better than copying someone else's, as it will have your energy imprint and not theirs; however, I have provided some examples below to get you started.

If we start our journey around the body with the hips, anatomically we know that they carry the weight of the upper body, and that their function is to allow us to move forward through their natural range of movement. If someone is rigid in their thinking, and this is stopping them from moving forward for whatever reason, according to the law of metaphysics, the hips will start to seize and become painful, ultimately becoming unable to perform their function.

An affirmation for healthy hips might be: I have an open mind, and allow myself to move forward in life, gracefully and confidently.

A poor example would be: 'My hips don't hurt anymore', or, 'I have no more pain and restriction in my hips'. In a strange quirk of the brain, it fails to 'compute' certain words. These words include: no, not, and don't, so it is best, in general, to avoid using these words, unless you are really determined to make changes and want to attract the universe's attention full on!

Instead of affirming that your hips don't hurt anymore, what your brain hears and responds to is 'My hips hurt more!' Equally, the second example would translate as, 'I have more pain and restriction in my hips'.

Keep to the positive words and begin your affirmation with statements such as, 'I am', 'I have', 'I now receive', 'I attract', 'My life is', 'I enjoy', and so on.

Empower your affirmation by repeating it at least three times in succession with genuine feeling, desire, and believability, like a mantra. You can repeat the empowering affirmation as many times as you like during your day, the more the better. If it is emotional healing that you are looking for, say your affirmation repeatedly while in the shower, allowing the water (which represents the emotion element within us) to cleanse you.

The secret behind getting results with affirmations is that you have to believe 100 per cent in what you seek and that it can come about. Saying the affirmation with conviction and passion helps bring faster results. If working with your health is too big to start with, think about something less monumental, like having a positive day. Your affirmation to say when you wake up in the morning could be something like, 'Today is already a wonderful day', or 'I welcome and thank this day for all its joy, happiness, and fulfillment'. Repeat this affirmation as you get ready for work and throughout the day, and notice how things unfold.

The other component to a successful affirmation is to trust that the passage to your intended goal is unfolding, even though it may not take the route you expect. This means that in order to achieve and enjoy that which you are affirming, you might need to clear some personal clutter, adjust your long-held views, and welcome the opportunities that present themselves as challenges so you can learn something important. This allows you to truly benefit fully from your life. If you remember that our health is a reflection of our inner beliefs, mindsets, and responses to life events, then you'll understand that if we continue to hold the same ingrained views, we are not going to be able to repair the corresponding health representation.

SOUL WHISPERING

*Your soul is ethereal, shapeless, and of gossamer
quality. It slips silently between lives,
revealing its voice so growth can prevail.*

*I*n our age of instant gratification and high-speed delivery, we
are often disappointed when the results we seek are not waiting for
us on the doorstep the morning following a session of affirmation
setting. It takes dedication, belief, and a bit of time to obtain results.
Remember, it took time to create the condition from which you now
wish to be released! Along the way, make sure you notice the small
gains, and do not dismiss them as meaningless. Doing this tells your
soul that you are not paying attention and that you are not grateful
unless the change is instant and astoundingly transformational.

There are other examples of how the skeleton's functions mirror
our emotions, beliefs, and meaningful events in our life at any given
time. Consider the spine, which serves to support the whole structure
of the body; if we feel unsupported in life or have received a severe
emotional blow, such as the loss of a best friend or partner, then it is
not uncommon for us to suffer sudden back problems from this loss
of support.

An affirmation for back problems would be: Life supports me in
everything I do. I trust in my own inner strength.

Neck and shoulder pain and stiffness reflect a strong sense of
duty that can result in the sufferer (or martyr) feeling that they are
carrying the world on their shoulders. This generally means that this
person is taking responsibility for others' problems and not letting
them resolve and learn from their own issues. This situation does
not let the souls of either party to grow, and comes from a basis of
neediness and control.

An affirmation for neck and/or shoulder problems: I release the need to carry others and their problems. I am flexible and creative in my thinking. I allow others to be responsible for their own lives.

Problems with the arms in general reflect a lack of willingness to embrace life and all it has to offer. Often, this affects people who feel stuck in life, a relationship, or a job they may be good at but which does not nourish their soul.

An affirmation for arms: I embrace all life has to offer. I am willing to accept change as a healthy and natural part of my life.

Problems with the legs, similar to the hips, show a lack of forward momentum in life, and can even become so stagnant and unable to move forward that the life does not progress at all.

An affirmation for legs in general would be: I confidently move forward in life. Every step I take brings me closer to my true purpose.

Problems with the knees reflect pride and also moving forward.

An affirmation for knees specifically would be: I am grateful for all opportunities to learn more about myself, and I accept these lessons with grace.

Problems with the smaller joints of the wrists, hands, ankles, and feet indicate specific pockets of cement-like thinking that has been held for a very long time. This might include consistent thoughts like, 'I have to work hard to be a worthy person', or 'if I look constantly busy, people will think I have important things to do, and that I am important'. It's all a bit of a game really, but it is what keeps many of us going! Hence, the corresponding condition of arthritic joints may manifest in these types of people.

An Affirmation for these areas would be: I release all rigid thinking and allow myself to be open-minded, free from judgment and welcoming of positive opportunities to grow.

SOUL WHISPERING

Release the need for control and allow your soul to show you what it feels like to soar.

*D*isease of the organs reflects specific emotions and beliefs about ourselves, rather than attitudes and beliefs about the outside world, which the skeleton houses. Founded on ancient Oriental observation, modern understanding of the mind-body connection validates what has been practiced for thousands of years in the East.

Every organ has its own signature emotion, which, if allowed to accumulate, causes ill health. Remember that the soul speaks through emotion and the body listens to every word you say! This is its currency, and the measure of our inner wisdom and learning. To the eternal core of you, everything is energy and there is nothing as consistently powerful as an emotion, particularly ones that are strongly held for a long time. As mentioned above, it has now been proven that every emotion triggers a chemical response in the body that finds its target cells, and upon so doing, latches onto it and starts to alter its functioning and constitution.

In dealing with numerous clients who have found their current emotional circumstances in need of consultation and guidance, the ancient philosophies have been proven time and time again in my experience. To help bring clarity and understanding to this concept, I have listed the organs below in association with the range of emotions that cause disharmony and ultimately disease within them.

Ailments of the liver focus around unresolved issues of deep frustration, anger, and even rage. It is commonly known in the therapy world that depression is often caused by a deep-seated anger that has no release and so has turned inwards to become a seething, smoldering cauldron that bubbles but cannot boil over. I have witnessed that problem drinkers are often trying to put out the fire caused by the rage of anger. Because alcohol affects the liver and long-term use can cause disease, these two adversaries are often engaged in a fight to the death.

To soften and release this negative emotion, affirm: I release all unserving emotions. I act in grace without judgment of others. I am patient and understanding. I am flexible and resilient yet strong, like bamboo. So, without strain, I allow myself to bend and flow with life.

The liver's associated organ is the gall bladder, and its emotional representative is bitterness. Gall stones represent crystallised events that continue to resonate, even with a quiet voice. It is common that someone suffering with a gall bladder condition has had to be very tolerant in their time. However, because they are also human, they have harboured unspoken resentments that have lead to bitterness.

To ease the impact on the gall bladder and start to release these emotions, affirm: I dissolve all outdated thinking and energetically release trapped words about others and myself, and employ gratitude for my blessings in this life.

The heart is the most exhaustively challenged organ because it continually seeks to maintain a balanced state of joy. Too much joy, as in the case of high blood pressure, can have very real and detrimental effects. Lack of joy, on the other hand, represented by low blood pressure and stagnation in the blood vessels, shows that the person has experienced a prolonged period of unhappiness and having to make do with what they see as their 'lot' in life. The heart is also adversely affected by alcohol consumption, again, used in an attempt to 'drown the nagging voice which speaks of the lack of joy', and this is why many alcoholics suffer from heart problems.

The heart holds pure soul energy. The emotions arising from and affecting this organ are joy and love. When we speak of love, we are not just concerned with finding it, having it fill our life, and giving it to others. We must also remember to give it to ourselves. In fact, this is the first and truest expression of love that is the foundation of what we hope to give to others. If we can't honestly love ourselves, how can we know what it feels like in order to extend love genuinely to another person?

To increase one's heart energy, affirm: Joy is abundant in my life. I am willing to be kind to myself. I release the need to deprive myself of self-love. I am both lovable and loved.

The small intestine, which is physically responsible for absorbing nutrients for the rest of the body to use, is the home of what I call 'external' fear. This means that when life presents challenges that are in some way threatening, such as a test, interview, or confrontation, we feel it in the 'gut'. Remember that the cells that ultimately become the two distinct halves of the heart originally were derived from the same cells that created the small intestine, so what affects one will naturally affect the other.

To increase one's heart energy, affirm: Joy is abundant in my life.

To strengthen the function of the small intestine, affirm: I confidently meet and successfully respond to all challenges. Today provides another opportunity to be creative, resourceful, and capable.

Next is the stomach, the home of dread. This is why we feel 'butterflies' in the stomach when we are particularly nervous or excited. In the short term, in conjunction with adrenaline, this serves to ensure that we operate at peak performance. In the long run, however, if this is our core personality emotion, it can lead to poor digestion, heartburn, and stomach ulcers.

To quell this emotion, affirm: I successfully manage this situation to its best possible outcome. I trust in myself. The universe supports me. I am confident and capable.

The spleen is the companion to the stomach in that it responds to the barrages of stress. Statistics have shown without doubt that what we call 'stress' is the number one trigger for numerous health problems. When we are stressed for a long time, we start to suffer common ailments such as mouth ulcers and colds. If the spleen's energy is further depleted, the rest of the body looses one of its main guardians against serious illness. Someone who leads a highly stressful life will ride the seesaw of dread and stress until their body can take it no longer. This is often when the heart steps in to make the distinct lack of joy known, and this is when some people experience the first awareness of heart problems that if left unattended at the cause may lead to a serious health event.

To release yourself from this cycle, any, some, or all of these affirmations may be helpful: My life is in balance. I am willing to release any unhelpful obligations, behaviours, and responsibilities. I am calm. I am relaxed. I know when to delegate. I trust and listen to my inner wisdom. I know my boundaries. I listen to my health and respond with relaxation, creativity, and time-out.

The pancreas deals with sugar metabolism. I see this as the forgotten treasure in therapy work, because it is through this organ that healing energy is magnified. In relation to life, the energy of this organ aligns with our ability, without acting selfishly, to put ourselves first when the time is right. It reflects how we honour ourselves with the 'sweets and treats' in life, and how we let ourselves enjoy life. It suffers when we continually sacrifice our own fulfillment for the benefit of others.

It has been noted that women who habitually put others' needs before their own, and deny themselves even the simplest pleasures, often embellish themselves with jewellery to excess, a bit like wanting all the candies in the shop. They seem to make up for their self-sacrificing nature through these external rewards. Men, on the other hand, surround themselves with 'boy toys', such as cars, boats, and motorcycles. Both of these behaviours are intended to make up for the lack of inner pleasure they cannot generate through recognition of their self-worth. Their measure of self-worth is represented in the (perceived) value of their trinkets. In physical terms, this may be the precursor to a person developing a condition such as diabetes.

To assuage these unhelpful emotions, affirm daily: I am lovable. I am worthy of recognition for who I am at this very moment. I am a reflection of the divine.

Start with simple requests. Perhaps your partner or boss asks you to 'just' do this little favour. If you know that it is going to cause you extra stress, or mean that something that something meaningful to you will be neglected, you could establish a boundary by saying, nicely of course, 'I could do what you ask, however, my time is already committed right now'. Really, if this favour is truly so small and will only 'just' take a few minutes to do, why is it being passed your way?

Often we let our boundaries get blurred because we want to help others and be seen as a kind and thoughtful person. There is absolutely nothing wrong in this, and I endorse this outlook 100 per cent. However, be mindful of individuals who continually will take advantage of your better nature for their benefit and learn to say, 'No!' To nurture self-worth, clear boundaries of acceptable behaviour need to be established and maintained. The more you are clear and employ these invisible markers of self-worth, the easier it becomes, and you will notice that the respect you have for yourself and your time is recognised by those around you.

Most of us hang on to clutter, whether physically, emotionally, mentally, or spiritually. This type of burden leads to the congestion of the energy of the large intestine, which has the emotional role to help us 'let go and move on' from the 'rubbish' of the past. Eight out of ten British citizens suffer from constipation at some point. While this is hardly a reason to rush to the doctor, it does represent a serious need clear some internal clutter, not only for the good of your health, but also your thinking and emotional reservoir. How can you move forward if you are hanging on to old thinking, arguments, and beliefs that no longer serve you? Releasing these outdated thoughts and freeing yourself to live in the present moment is like taking a decongestant for the soul!

Affirmations to clear the energy of the large intestine include: I move easily and comfortably with the flow of life. I let go of outdated thinking, arguments, and beliefs, and I send them away with thanks and gratitude. I am whole and complete within myself.

The lungs are the residence of grief, and accommodate the abundant tears that one may cry on the inside – they are there to soak them up. When the large intestine becomes congested, its mucus fluids migrate upward to the waiting, sponge-like lungs, which soak up all this moisture until they can't cope any longer and a medical condition results. This is often experienced as asthma.

Basically, any condition where the lungs are compromised suggests that the sufferer is reluctant to fully engage in life because they are unable, or perhaps, for whatever reason, unwilling to fully take in the breath of life. Deep grief can result not only from bereavement, but also from any significant loss that resonates deeply with the individual.

To help strengthen the lung's energy, affirm: I fully engage in life. I am safe, supported, and comforted with every breath. I open myself to fully enjoy life and all it has to offer. I take sensible risks and am successfully rewarded.

We move now to the kidneys. Located on either side of the spine, these organs are the seats of our vitality. They hold our lifetime of energy and act as a storehouse for all our liveliness and vigour. Their emotion is fear. This is different from the 'external' fear of the small intestine. It is, instead, an 'internal' fear, wherein a person views and responds to the world around them and even simple events in their life as though they were a threat, and as though something bad might happen at any moment. They often carry the 'rabbit caught in the headlights' look, and are overly cautious in almost every circumstance. This excessive expenditure of energy rapidly uses up their kidneys' vitality, meaning that they find themselves easily tired, lacking true freedom and joy (which ultimately reflects in and on the heart), and prone to premature aging!

For the vitality of the kidneys, affirm: Life supports me. I am safe. I trust in myself. I trust the universe to guide, care for, and nurture me. All is well.

The bladder completes the list of the main organ's emotional hosting, as we now consider the effects of anxiety and annoyance. Constantly harbouring these emotions yields conditions like cystitis.

The bladder would benefit from affirmations such as: I release all irritations and let life flow around and through me. I direct my energy toward positive thoughts and emotions. I release all anxiety. I am calm and centred.

Ailments concerning the reproductive organs, in general, represent a need to extend the energy of self-love, self-acceptance, and creativity. The process of stifling our reproductive energy begins when we are told that we are not creative. This can happen in art class, music lessons, woodworking, domestic science class, and any environment where we endeavour in our formative years to make something from our own creative juices. We are labeled or label ourselves uncreative, the energy of our self-expression starts to wane. Add to this the early fumblings of intimacy, and the scene is further set.

This is also the place of our mother-self connection.

This is also the place of our mother-self connection. It is astounding how many women have experienced some form of sexual abuse, let alone perhaps grown up in an environment that degrades and devalues their femininity and role as a valuable contributor to society. With the nurturing energy severed to the reproductive organs, it is no wonder that conditions such as fibroids, endometriosis, and uterus and breast cancer are rife. In contrast, for most men – although the incidence of testicular cancer is more prevalent in the younger generations, perhaps as a reflection of conflicted roles and responsibilities – it is not until they reach their mid-sixties approximately, when they may feel that their masculine roles are not as strong as previously, that they typically suffer from common conditions affecting the prostate gland.

In either case, affirmations are an excellent way to honour ourselves for who we are, help to balance the energy, release old patterning and beliefs about our roles and increasing life and sexual pleasure.

Affirmations for the reproductive system in both men and women include: I fully embrace my sexuality and rejoice in my ability to honour myself. I release any and all limiting beliefs, expectations, and distorted ideas about my body, my sexuality, or my ability to enjoy meaningful relationships placed in my consciousness by any external source. I release any concepts that restrict my self-love. I am a creative person with a unique self-expression that is authentic to me. I attract only nurturing relationships that honour me as I am.

Finally, we turn to the brain, spinal cord, and nerve pathways of the body. This amazing communication system carries the energy and light of the body in pulses translated from the senses and signals from the organs. We develop ailments of this system when we are no longer able to communicate with the outside world and we retreat into ourselves. We can maintain a healthy nervous system and brain throughout our life by regularly removing ourselves from stress, pressure, and the demands of everyday living. Meditation, visualisation, music, mantras, chanting, and being in nature all refuel the brain and allow it to relax. When you are able to remove yourself from your stressors, try the following affirmation: I cope well with all demands, stresses, and requirements. I am me. I am free to be myself, and I communicate openly with my feelings and the outside world.

When we have let the balance of our life's activities centre on either physical work or intellectual progress, we find that the energy withdraws from that particular area as we age. Someone who has dedicated themselves to academic pursuits may find himself less capable in advancing years of engaging their minds in such a way. It is almost like they have given so much already, that they withdraw into their own world, which is easier and less demanding. People who have been tremendously physically active all their lives through their career or lifestyle do the same by withdrawing physically and perhaps becoming less mobile. This is, of course, a tremendously simplistic way of looking at these situations; however, it is intended to offer a glimpse of what the soul is yearning for after a lifetime of responding to the free will of its host and its own progress along its soul journey.

Affirmations may be useful here where possible. The most powerful one is: I am comfortable in myself. I am loved, supported, and well cared for. I am grateful for my life.

In understanding the impact of our emotions, beliefs, attitudes, and experiences on the energy of our body, we can take a greater responsibility for the journey of our health, which ultimately is a direct reflection of our soul. If we act for our highest good, which means in the highest interest of our soul, then recognising early what is potentially damaging to our health is surely a valuable tool.

I have experienced change and total transformation, both personally and through the lives of my clients, brought about by honouring the messages that pulse through our daily lives. Ultimately, take a look at your health, but don't scare yourself. If there is something that concerns you, visit your doctor as a natural first step. The affirmations are given to support you toward improved health on all levels. Work with them regularly, alongside whatever other approaches seem right and responsible. When you start to forget to say them, they have begun to have an effect!

CHAPTER 6

Finding Inner Peace

CHAPTER 6

Finding Inner Peace

Be still and listen. Be still and learn. Be still and be free.

$\mathcal{I}$n this world of highflying living and the constant demands of modern-day Western existence, it is all too often forgotten that part of creating balance in our lives is to simply be still. In so doing, we can start to acquaint ourselves with what is necessary to achieve inner peace, and ultimately this can resonate from our very core as a tangible quality of our character. For many of us, what we crave as an antidote to our harsher life experiences can turn into a manic pursuit and actually congest the very goal we are trying to achieve.

The inner peace many of us seek does not come from 'switching off' and sitting in front of the television for a few hours, or even reading a book. (It's okay, though. Don't stop. Keep reading, and my intention is that you will be better for it!) So, what, then, is inner peace?

Inner peace radiates from in a deep well within the heart and is the domain of the soul. Traditionally in the Far East, one practices daily to generate and sustain this deep connection. And yet, we need not dedicate our entire lives to this pursuit in order to receive the benefits. In our own way, if we take the time, we can start to enjoy the rewards of health and happiness from this highly important component of learning to listen to your soul.

If the art of knowing your inner peace was described using the senses, it would be something like this: It is transparent, like a sweet yet herby fragrance drifting unexpectedly on the gentlest of breezes that had been warmed by the uninterrupted glow of the radiant sun. It would carry the sound of delicate wind chimes mixed perfectly with the melody of bird song at sunrise. There would be the taste of your favourite meal lingering on your taste buds. But most of all, your sense of touch would be ignited as you felt the tender caresses around your shoulders, as though you had just received a comforting hug from a magnificent angel.

SOUL WHISPERING

I whisper to you in ways that you would recognize, through something that has meaning to you. Look, listen, feel, and see. It is all there already around you. I always have been.

*I*nner peace is a feeling. It is knowledge. It is a place deep within you that is carried with you wherever you go, and you can connect immediately with it in an instant. It is a freedom from negative emotions that frustrate your efforts to be healthy, happy, and whole. It hosts great wisdom and effortlessly allows you to connect with your true self.

115

It carries no expectation or obligation. It simply is.

We have all been hardwired with some degree of work ethic, with a sense of duty, values, and morality, and the need for completeness that we usually think can only come from finding a partner and, more often as not, procreating, without ever asking ourselves if this is really what we want. The fervent pursuit of anything – family, career, wealth, free time – can be all consuming, and is the very thing that can erode inner peace faster than a corrosive chemical.

Most of our modern, goal-oriented pursuits sacrifice this greatest treasure that can offer us solace, retreat, and sanctuary when we need it most. Many of us work tremendously hard to give ourselves a better life and more freedom, and yet we cannot answer the question, 'What is enough?' The aim, if we subscribe to this formula, is to get ourselves to a point where by we have enough money, security, homes, and love from a partner and family to give us the time, space, and tranquility to enjoy our life. Ironically, what we seek has been within us all the time; it has just been silenced through our trivial, external pursuits. If we are lucky, we can, at some point, eventually settle back and relish the very things that have been with us all the time, which we thought were out there somewhere. This is when one can find inner peace.

How much of your day is occupied in thinking, planning, doing, or reacting? I would imagine that it is most of it, am I right? So if this is the case, how much of your day is given over to just being? Not a lot, if you are like most people! Not if you have a career, family or partner, responsibilities, or ambitions. This is only natural in today's world, and you are not to blame. However, since everything we experience is governed by the choices we make, then there exists an opportunity to understand more about the value of attaining inner peace, and this is a choice you are free to make at any time. There is no special equipment required, no classes to attend, no memberships, no textbooks full of special techniques – just a simple decision to make the time, even for a few minutes each day, to still yourself and be free from movement or mental momentum. No doubt you will be restless at first. However, with a little practice, your day will not feel complete without it.

SOUL WHISPERING

Inner peace is achieved by self-acceptance,
self-honouring, forgiveness,
and above all self-love.

*I*nner peace is a solid, all-encompassing, not sacrificial, state of being. We can embrace this quality and yet be highly involved in our everyday life. We do not have to change our careers, leave our homes, travel lonely and difficult journeys, abandon our loved ones, donate the children's inheritance to a special organization, or take ourselves off to a mountaintop to meditate for the next twenty years. Because we have already established that it is our free will that allows us to make these choices, we could do any number of these things if we felt so inclined, and if it helped our progress, then fair enough.

However, consider this fact: Because you host a soul that has seen many lifetimes and learned a great deal already, you were born fully capable of creating and building upon your own inner peace. This was a fact long before you took your first steps and before you accumulated anything in the outside world of any perceived value. Remember that you are here to learn more about being human. Remain on the path, and do not pre-empt the journey by detaching from reality in the name of your spiritual quest. You are here for a reason.

The possibility of attaining total inner peace lies dormant, patiently awaiting its wake-up call in every cell of your body. When it is released, it directs its wealth of feelings through the heart, which acts as a coordinator so that you can appreciate its power. From this energetic hub, the sense of deep inner peace is honoured, and therefore further empowered, until it silences any and all negative voices that harp on about past events.

If we lack inner peace, we react rather than respond. We judge before we are judged. We can give criticism but cannot take it. We surround ourselves with 'this week's close friends', and then dispense with them when they do not follow our command or fail to meet our ever-shifting expectations. We condemn others for their actions in order to draw attention away from what we perceive to be our own shortcomings. We might rise to the top of the ladder, but we will have broken every rung along the way. Ultimately, although we can live a life without answering the call for inner peace, it is often one that is embattled with repetitive circumstances that all try to hold a mirror to our soul as it cringes in response to the behaviour of the spirit it partners with for this lifetime.

I once knew someone who was, on the outside, a very difficult person to be around. Nothing was ever enough, or good enough. Life was certainly a trial, not a journey. If your manners or ideas did not fit, then you were dumped. If you tried to be nice and friendly, you were seen as weak, and this led to you being manipulated and taken advantage of without hesitation or restraint. And yet, when you could catch the odd glimpse of the true person underneath, there was a loving, creative, special individual just yearning for companionship and love. The bit that was missing was inner peace. This person was very intelligent, the life of the party, artistically gifted, strong minded, and a high scholarly achiever, but sadly was emotionally damaged in early childhood. This early experience effected the formation of their ideas about life and how to avoid being unfairly treated again.

Everything initiated from that decisive tender moment. The world they created and how they responded to relationships, circumstances, and people in general was essentially a child's response to a situation originally out of their control, which they continued to choose to rule their behaviour. This quite small event had hardwired this persons thinking forever in this lifetime.

For this person, as the decades rolled on, the mindset became concrete, producing further incidences that added cement. Without realising it, they were still trying to win the battle they had lost as a child, which, of course, could never be won. Had this person gone beyond just reading the books about personal development and actually practiced some of the techniques, perhaps some seeds might have started to take root. If they had been able to let go of the incident in their childhood and release their anger and rigid thinking, inner peace would have started to flow, and its effects would have been more harmonious relationships, lasting friendships and a richly enjoyable life in every respect. Sadly, this never came to pass in this lifetime. Although their soul may have learned other lessons, in this regard this soul will need to address this lesson in the future, when it returns to Earth, the school for souls.

Developing a strong link with your inner peace allows you to first of all forgive the people, circumstances, events, and most importantly yourself for the less desirable experiences, words, decisions, actions, or choices that are now in the past. Remember that you can learn from every experience. If you think to look at what you could learn from an event that requires forgiveness and accept the lesson, this is the first step towards truly embracing forgiveness and claiming your inner peace.

If we learn what we live, then if we can generate our own infinite source of inner peace, we will then be able to positively influence many others during our lifetime.

Your soul's message: Finding inner peace is like finding the thread that weaves through all your experiences, creating a rich and nourishing tapestry of your life.

Inner peace is the natural character of a contented soul. When we carry the weight of the past and hold others to blame, we have trouble trusting anyone, including ourselves. We may not form or keep friendships very easily. We may not take responsibility for our actions. We may always try to set the balance straight, and regardless of whether the original incident or offender is long gone, we hold ourselves in a place of perpetual readiness and alert, looking for any opportunity to redress the situation to our favour.

SOUL WHISPERING

Forgiveness does not mean that you accept, condone, or welcome the same actions again.

*H*ow do you forgive? First of all, since considering forgiving a person or yourself can be a huge undertaking, you might need to start off by simply being willing to forgive. Or even be willing to be willing to forgive! Take a few days if you need to, and get used to the idea of starting the forgiving process. Imagine what your life would be like if the energy you currently put into holding anger, hurt, resentment, or any other negative or limiting emotion was returned to you to help enhance your life. You may come to realise that a large part of your personality and reality framework on which you base decisions, respond to events, and choose your relationships is influenced by your lack of forgiveness, and therefore your lack of inner peace.

If the idea of removing this large chunk of yourself seems too big or frightening, then consider what you could use to fill the newly created void. Ultimately, it is inner peace that will fill the chasm. However, as we transit towards this ideal, some people take on a creative project to give themselves something they can be satisfied with when it is finished. This can help increase self-esteem, self-worth, and confidence. Others spend more time with family and friends, building stronger relationships with those who mean so much to them. Above all, the most important way of redirecting the energy that would otherwise have been spent holding onto the past is to focus on creating a better relationship with yourself. This means that you stop criticising yourself and avoid self-limiting beliefs and behaviour. You send a message to yourself that you are a good person and that you deserve all the joy, happiness, and fulfillment life can offer.

Some people take on a creative project to give themselves something they can be satisfied with when it is finished.

Basically, to generate solid inner peace, you need to practice unconditional love, both of and for yourself. This does not mean that you should become arrogant and conceited. It simply means that you should always think, behave, and respond to life in a way that honours the wonderful, special, and limitless soul that you are.

SOUL WHISPERING

When your soul smiles it lights up the world around you.

*Y*ou need not start with the biggest thing that needs forgiveness. You could 'practice' on much smaller events and issues. Get used to how good this feels. As you progress, you will sense inner peace and compassion beginning to fill your heart.

Forgiveness is sign of strength, not weakness. Before you extend your solvent graciousness, first learn from the event so that you do not attract, and therefore repeat, the experience again. You might sit in front a blank piece of paper and complete the following sentence: 'Before I extend forgiveness in relation to X, and let it go, I realise that I have learned Y from this situation...' Do this for each situation or person for which you hold negative emotions where forgiveness could be offered. To get an idea of how much hold the lack of forgiveness has on you, try this: How does it feel if you imagine that you have already offered the necessary forgiveness? Notice your thoughts and feelings when you say, 'Now that I have forgiven X, I feel...'

When you feel comfortable with this initial concept, engage the second awareness of the forgiveness act. This means that, for whatever reasons the act of forgiving might be employed, it does not imply that you accept or would welcome again the actions, words, influence, or repeated involvement of that particular person, or your own behaviour, in your life again.

Forgiveness is an absolute. Once you have genuinely extended it, you do not have to tender to its maintenance. The act of forgiving does not absolve you or any one else from the responsibility for your actions or to act honourably in future. Whether you need to forgive yourself or another, what it means to do so is that you are willing to let go of the emotional burden or pain that has been caused. This is naturally often difficult to do; however, the weight of emotion that can be removed is often not appreciated until it has been released.

The additional impact of holding someone in the light of forgiveness will ensure that his or her soul receives this message, and in doing so, they will be encouraged to release the patterns of behaviour that caused the problem in the first place. Imagine if we could all send forgiveness to those who have angered, harmed, hurt, betrayed, or damaged us in some way. What a release this would be, and what a positive impact there would be on all of humanity!

Once you have initially unburdened yourself, you will be able to sift though the other significant issues that require your attention using the same method. One by one, you will feel their influence diminish. As you start to be less burdened, your feelings of inner peace will naturally start to grow through your new soul connectedness. You will begin to smile more, laugh more, and find yourself feeling light-hearted. This 'new you' will radiate its clean, clear energy far and wide, and in response you will only attract the kind of people and experiences that reflect what you are radiating. This is true of whatever energy you extend, so this is why it is so important to establish inner peace through embracing forgiveness as one of your core soul strengths.

SOUL WHISPERING

My strength is your strength, and your weakness
is mine to heal; your turmoil is mine to quell,
and your life is mine to enrich.

*W*hen you invoke the benefits of inner peace your soul will breathe a sigh of relief and you will sense a deep calmness within. Compassion will naturally begin to germinate. For the purposes of its learning and ultimate growth, your soul agreed before it incarnated within you, to undergo the trials and events that would ultimately provide its required lessons for this lifetime and help build your character. It is the lessons that are the most important part of any event. Missing the lesson but holding onto the event is like winning the battle but losing the war! Many people experience hardship, struggle, deprivation and misery and falsely think that 'this is their lot' and that they are powerless to change anything.

It is easy to stay in this mindset if we do not expect to learn anything from our experiences. However, from the soul's perspective, every experience in one's life is an opportunity for growth and enrichment. Learning to forgive is one of the main growth factors of any soul and its host. Once forgiveness is mastered, fear is removed from our mindset because we know we are not held by the past and we can effectively create our future. Then we can embark on many different adventures mentally, emotionally and physically, as we know that there is something to be gained even from the simplest of events along the journey. When inner peace manifests, we are able to handle life's challenges with grace and wisdom. We float above the need to engage in the turmoil of guilt, blame, and excuses. We radiate this wonderful quality all around us.

While finding inner peace is largely about invoking forgiveness, it is also about centering yourself to listen to the messages from your soul. This, in itself, brings rich rewards regarding how to conduct your life, resolve difficult decisions, take the next step, and generally learn to accept and love yourself.

If you find yourself looking forward to a night at home alone, even if you live alone normally, then your soul may be talking to you and wanting you to take some time to be still and start to connect with your inner self.

To honour this calling, do what comes naturally. This may mean taking yourself away for a weekend alone – away from mobile phones, familiar faces, and commitments. It may involve staying at home, unplugging the phone, and having a long, hot, candle-lit bath. It may mean taking a nice walk in nature, or just being surrounded by beautiful music. If you are to be in a special or specific place, so be it. Take a notepad and pen, a bottle of water, and go! The process is quite simple.

I like to have a notebook and pen next to me when I am searching for answers in this way. Jot down a few questions, focusing on how best to connect with or establish your inner peace. Once settled, making sure you are in a safe setting where you won't be disturbed, close your eyes and focus on your breathing. After a few deep breaths, you may feel your heart rate slowing and your shoulders relaxing. When you are ready, hold a vision of a beautiful sunset in your mind's eye. Use your senses to enrich this vision. Focusing on something like this stops your mind chattering and trying to hijack you!

The first step to start to nurture your inner peace as you sit quietly is to just ask yourself, 'How best can I forgive X?' Take the first answer that comes. It will often be in your own voice. Do not discount it, and follow the guidance you receive to the best of your ability! Write down the messages as you get them for later reflection so that you don't have to remember anything and can focus on the act of being still and centred.

If you are having trouble getting started, you could say to yourself several times, 'I am now willing to forgive X, accept the learning arising from this situation, and move forward with my life. Please make me aware of the learning from this experience'. If you have more questions or if new ones arise, ask them in the same way and record your insights.

In todays hectic world the pursuit of inner peace may initially seem very illusive. In reality, it is actually quite easy to establish a rewarding practice intended to unite you with and nurture your inner peace. All it takes is a few moments of mindfullness each day. This can happen as you take your shower, walk to your office, eat your lunch, relax at the end of the day or even when you are about to drop off to sleep.

By taking just a few moments, breathing deeply and letting your physical, mental and emotional tensions get softer with very breath, you will start to reap the rewards very quickly. Using a simple affirmation like to one below can give your mind something to think about instead of the daily events.

If you want to connect with your inner peace, you could affirm the following:

'With everyday, deep within myself, I am growing calmer and more serene. My well of inner peace is infinite'.

If you find it difficult to get some time alone or away from your daily responsibilities, recite the intention below as you settle into bed at night. To help you start to open your heart to offering forgiveness and therefore moving yourself nearer to working with true compassion in your life, you might consider the power of the following words:

THE SOUL'S FORGIVENESS INTENTION

I embrace all experiences in the knowledge that I attract to myself that which will ensure my growth.

I am willing to hold myself up to the light for purification.

I am willing to forgive myself on all levels across all lifetimes.

I honour myself and value myself as a person of worth and a much-loved child of the universe.

I forgive (or am willing to think about forgiving) any and all others for their actions.

I release the need to cast blame.

In doing so, I thank any and all others for their willingness to help me grow.

I release myself from self-blame, guilt, and detriment.

I forgive (or am willing to think about forgiving) myself.

I act in grace and integrity as I forgive.

I release the past and move forward richer and more complete.

I forgive, therefore I am free and empowered to live authentically and abundantly in the present moment.

And so it is.

*I*f you are able to say these words, from the heart, at least once a day, you will start to notice subtle changes in a very short time. I find that the best time to do this is as you settle into bed at night. I keep a little notebook on my bedside table that contains this and other, similar soul-growth-oriented thoughts for easy reading. As you drift into sleep, the energy of this sentiment will stay with you and start to filter into your living and soul consciousness.

The soul responds literally, and will believe what you are affirming. This is why you must genuinely enforce your willingness. It won't take long before you start to feel the changes within you. Regular practice over just three weeks will initiate huge changes. Once you have practiced generating and connecting with your new-found core, others will notice the difference in you and may comment positively.

Your eyes will hold the reflection of your inner sanctuary. Your heart will send waves of acceptance and unconditional love in every direction, and yet you will only attract those who can 'read' your energy because they carry the same within them. How wonderful would life be if this were the norm for all of us?

BECKY'S AWAKENING

*B*ecky lived and worked in a hectic cosmopolitan city with buildings of concrete, glass, and steel. She rushed to work every morning, eating her breakfast on the way. She rarely took a lunch break, and was always quick to volunteer to stay late if the boss asked.

She enjoyed her job; however, she knew that she would not stay at this particular company for more than five years. Her boss saw how keen she was to work hard, and yet never truly appreciated the reasons for her willingness. This only made her work harder for some scrap of appreciation and recognition.

After one particularly bad flu virus, which had made her take a week off for bed rest, Becky came to see me because she felt that her life was out of control. We explored the messages her soul was trying to impart by looking at the challenges she was currently facing. It soon became obvious that it was not the twenty-nine-year-old professional that was seeking attention and recognition, but a young girl of only seven.

Becky's father, a very successful businessman, had brought her up with the concept that working hard made you a good person, and that this made you acceptable and valuable, worthy of being liked and loved. Becky had set this as her route to finding what she had missed during her childhood due to her parents' divorce, which was brought about by her father's career ambitions. She felt she had missed out on the fullness of her father's love, time, and attention. She loved her parent's dearly, yet she felt that they were at least partly responsible for her current lack of fulfillment.

By exploring the parallels between her past and present situations, it was Becky who immediately saw the similarities. We worked together through guided visualization to release her from her parents' mindset, so that she was able to learn, forgive them, and start to establish her own work ethic. Then, as home practice, we created some affirmations specifically for her situation. We worked to release the patterns that were blocking her inner peace, and brought her to a place where she no longer needed to seek external acceptance. Instead, she began to nurture herself from within. On her follow-up session two weeks later, she reported that she no longer rushed to work or missed her lunch hour, and only volunteered to work late if she could see that the rest of her week would be easier.

Because she was operating from her inner core of tranquility, she was more focused, and therefore actually achieved more in her normal working hours, which meant that she rarely had a backlog of work to cause her to stay behind. Her boss noticed how her efficiency had improved, how she no longer raced around the office in a blind panic, and that the number of errors she made had been reduced to virtually zero. He was so impressed that he recommended her for some advanced training and suggested that she should develop some guidelines for the junior staff members to help them become more organised and better time managers.

Becky could not deny that her workday was more pleasurable. She felt less pressured all together. She spent time each day sitting in nature and practicing the deep breathing that she knew would connect her with her inner peace. After a few weeks of practice, she positively radiated serenity and her face lit up when she smiled. When we last spoke, she informed me that she had decided to now be known as Rebecca, at work as well as to her family and friends. Few questioned this request; however, to those who did, her reply was confident and insightful: 'I am not the person I was when I was known as Becky [her familial 'pet' name]. Now I am the 'me' I have always wanted to be, and my old name doesn't suit me anymore!'

On the surface, this client came to me with a fairly fundamental problem that needed to be explored and reflected back to her. The tools we used suited her mindset perfectly because she was ready for a change. The degree of change was evident by her inner and outer transformation. Rebecca's flu virus could be seen as a message from her soul to give her the time to seek the transformation that she and her soul needed at that time. The soul knows the truth about what is important and meaningful to our growth. If we 'still' ourselves, we can benefit from its wisdom. Creating and connecting with our inner peace brings numerous benefits because it requires us to get our house in order.

The act of forgiveness is nourishing to the soul. When you begin to connect, your soul will lovingly guide you and make sure that you are gaining what you need at any given moment. You have the power within you to release old, useless emotions that hold you back in some negative way. Your life and world can start to change today. Take some quiet time; be still and connect; ask your questions; listen and grow. Your world of today will reflect the radiance of your inner peace. It costs nothing, yet is one of the routes to true wealth. Try it. It won't take long, and you will be in a very different place in a week or two – of that you can be sure.

CHAPTER 7

Sara's Story —
The Returnling

CHAPTER 7

Sara's Story – The Returnling

Everything happens in divinely right timing.

Some years ago, following a phase of personal exploration of forgiveness en route to strengthening my own inner peace, a new client made her way to me. I have always firmly believed that every client and student finds their way to my door at the most appropriate time for both of us and that I am only sent the most wonderful people! Equally, I believe that each of these special individuals brings with them both a need to learn and a lesson to impart. Therefore, we engage in a mutual exchange on a soul level. In this case, Sara's experiences are very valid, not only for their significance to her but also to me, and as usual, the timing was perfect.

A nurse in her late twenties, Sara had taken time off work lately following a miscarriage. This tragic event resulted from her having been knocked down by an out-of-control skateboarder as she was walking through a local park, following a check-up at a nearby hospital.

She had been six months pregnant at the time.

Sara began our initial visit by saying that she wanted to share a strange dream with me that she had had a few nights before. She claimed that she could remember all the details with amazing clarity. As she began, she apologised for needing to explain it exactly as it had happened. I was grateful for all the information she could share!

Ready to give her my full attention, I sensed my breathing slow and deepen, and I knew that my awareness was enhanced. As I listened intently, she shared her experience.

'I believe my baby came to me in a dream', Sara began. 'My mind flooded with questions. Something told me that my baby wanted to speak with me and that I might not get another chance to do so. I barely noticed that I was in an unfamiliar, yet comfortable, luminescent landscape. Everything seemed very still, although there were many other people moving around and gathering in groups, chatting without noticing my arrival.

'I felt the vague beginnings of a connection, even though I could only sense a presence. I knew this was an encounter to savour. "Start off slow," I cautioned myself. Then I asked, into the void immediately to my left, where I sensed 'someone' waiting to speak to me, feeling somewhat nervously excited, "Do you have a name?"

'There was a pause before the faint, almost reluctant, yet warm reply. "You can call me Joseph".

'It was amazing. A boy! I knew it! A rush went through me before I asked, consciously trying to match my companion's tone without sounding too demanding, "Can I see what you look like?"'

Sara was very animated by this point. She continued to clearly recall every detail of her night-time encounter.

"'There is no need for you to see me. I only take on a flesh form when it's time to manifest', Joseph replied somewhat cryptically. 'For now, imagine me as pure white light'. Then, without being prompted, he continued. 'When you centre yourself, you can feel me in the "stillness in your heart between each heartbeat."'"

SOUL WHISPERING

To connect with your soul, be still and listen to the wisdom that radiates from your heart. It knows your truth and will always guide you for your best interests. The secret is to be still and listen, and then to have the courage to trust and act on the messages you receive.

'These words brought a tangible wave of comfort', Sara continued. 'Although I was asleep, I vaguely remember involuntarily placing my hands on my heart-centre, in the middle of my chest, as I connected with the feeling. I felt myself smile from inside. Then, in a gentle appeal, I asked, "Why didn't you stay? Why did you have to leave like you did?"

'I knew my burdened question betrayed my feelings of loss and guilt, but I waited, as I have done so many times before when I have pleaded into the emptiness of the night. However, this time I was anticipating an answer. The silence was painful. For a while, I thought I had lost the connection'.

Sara paused to check that I was still 'with' her. I could say nothing at this point, as there was clearly more she needed to share. She was starting to show signs of her loss her eyes, which were brimming with tears, as she drew strength and continued.

'Then Joseph's voice said, "It was already decided".

'Disheartened by the response, I persisted, unwilling to let this moment pass. "Did you have a choice about whether to stay or leave?" I queried, hoping for an answer that would bring me some understanding.

'Again, it seemed like an eternity before I received another reluctant reply, yet I sensed that the relationship between myself and my never-to-be-born child had a definite familiarity and was getting stronger.

'There was an air of understanding within his words that I found both unnerving and yet reassuring at the same time. It was as if I was talking to one of my favourite old school teachers, whom I trusted. Joseph had great patience, and seemed to be used to predictable questions from people like me. Yet this was, or rather would have been, my baby – my lifelong charge, who would have been so vulnerable and defenseless for the first stages of his life. How had I now arrived at this moment of knowing that he could provide me with answers?'

Sara looked directly at me as she asked the question, but continued without waiting for an answer. She wondered if Joseph would offer some words that might ease the feelings of blame and grief that she had carried since the pain had ripped through her on that fateful September afternoon. It was obvious that Sara treasured and trusted this contact.

Since the accident, she explained, she had only experienced fleeting wisps of this presence during her day and nighttime dreams, or sometimes when she meditated. On these occasions, she had always noticed that her surroundings had seemed to become much brighter, almost as if there had been a soft light source radiating in the room, even when she focused her attention at night when the room was almost dark. She then continued with the story of her experience.

'"It was not a matter of choice," Joseph explained, soft with tenderness, considering the words he was about to deliver. "I was never meant to manifest as your son".

'Somewhat bewildered, I blurted, "What?" With that, I must have half-awoken Eddy, my husband, and I nearly jolted myself from my own deep sleep. "What do you mean, never meant to manifest?" I asked. I am afraid I must have sounded demanding. I was startled and slightly angry, given everything I had been through'.

Sara drew breath as she perched on the edge of her chair. Joseph had withdrawn and returned to the realms of the seraphic mist.

'I was now fully disturbed from my sleep, and as I lay perfectly still, barely breathing, I was conscious of my heart pounding beneath my hands. Then I became aware of an unfamiliar, however very real and comforting feeling radiating from my heart-centre. It felt as though my heart was wide open, like a beautiful lotus blossom that radiated a gentle fragrance in tangible waves extending far beyond me. There was also a warm feeling in the same place, which I naturally wanted to keep hold of, so I remained very still. Motionless, I recalled every detail of this most-treasured encounter, and berated myself for prematurely ending the contact. "Can I call him back?" I thought. "Please, please, come back. I'm sorry. Please...." Even though I tried for what seemed like an eternity, the gnawing disappointment became overwhelming when nothing happened'.

Sara described how she spent the remainder of the dark, silent hours recalling the conversation. She was now totally consumed in gaining confirmation that the connection she was feeling deep within her was real. The expanded feeling radiating from her heart continued. At the same time, she acknowledged her awareness of the chorus of other emotions that played like a tune that is annoyingly lodged in the mind. Mimicking her dream, she continued to hold her hands clasped at her heart-centre as she slumped back in her chair, now finished telling her story.

'Can you tell me why Joseph was not meant to manifest?' Sara asked me.

I sensed a deeper well of serenity occupying my mind and body as I found myself looking directly into Sara's heart through her eyes. I began to deliver the message that was being given to me.

'The fact that you can recall your dream so clearly shows that you were most likely astral travelling', I began. 'This means that you were visiting a different reality while you slept. This is confirmed by the fact that you could recall every detail more than twenty minutes after awaking.

'In the safety of your sleep, you were having an out-of-body experience. Everything you experienced was totally real, and yet was happening in a different dimension. Many people experience this without realising what it is. Memories of these experiences can stay with you for years. When you travel to the astral plane, you receive the chance to learn about yourself and access information that might otherwise not be available to you. This type of experience can enhance your thinking and, ultimately, if you pay attention to what you experience, it may positively influence the rest of your life. There is obviously a reason why Joseph did not manifest, and also why he decided to contact you in this way.

'It seems that the soul of your baby took this opportunity to call to you so that he could help you move forward. Remember that the soul is an eternal and quintessential energy signature that is an intangible, yet guiding force within all living things. It is not uncommon for souls to help others in this way.

'When we are asleep we have fewer barriers in place, and access to us is easier and safer. Some people, if they find the content of such 'dreams' too much to cope with, might dismiss them without exploring their significance. However, their inner wisdom tells them that they should pay attention to the messages available. In these cases, the universe will find other ways to tell them what they need to be aware of until they finally 'listen'.

'From a soul's perspective, you must understand, a lifetime is not measured by the number of years lived, how much money is accumulated, how big one's house is, or by ego-driven achievements, but rather by the learning that is gained or imparted. Before every soul returns to Earth, it reviews its previous lives. With the help of its guides and mentors, it decides what it needs and wants to learn from its next visit'.

Sara listened intently, not feeling the need to question at this stage.

'Upon defining its learning mission', I continued, 'the returning soul seeks approval from the Universal Council of Elders who govern all souls. When agreement is granted, the soul undertakes a contract that highlights its intended purpose in the next lifetime. From there, the search begins for suitable cellular hosts, here on Earth, the "soul school". Every soul has its own agenda, and chooses when and where to reconnect based on the experiences to be gained by aligning with the path of its 'parents', culture, environment, challenges, and ultimately the likelihood of it achieving its contracted goals.

'Some returning souls are reluctant to take on a new life because of the experiences they have had in a previous one, or in some cases because they know what is in store for them. As a soul's purpose is to ultimately experience all facets of being human, it needs to return numerous times in a wide variety of settings and circumstances before it can reach enlightenment, and then ascend to serve humanity on a greater scale.

'The incoming soul understands the spirit of the person it is to unite with and become, so that together their journey has substance. The soul then has the opportunity to linger near its host's family for a while to make sure that it has made the right choice before conception occurs. When the time is appropriate, the soul starts to make its journey toward its host. In some cases, the parents subconsciously sense this presence and describe 'knowing' that a baby is on its way. In other instances, young children in the family can sense this incoming energy. This generally happens about three to four months beforehand, when the energy of the mother, the father, and the soul start to align'.

Sara jolted to attention, recalling that a few months prior to discovering that she was pregnant, their three-year-old daughter, Laura, had announced that she was making a box full of toys for the 'new baby'. She talked regularly of the new arrival, and even before the pregnancy was confirmed, would chatter away to Sara's growing belly, as though she already knew this infant. Sara had completely forgotten about her daughter's seemingly innocent behaviour until just then. Strangely, Laura stopped mentioning the baby a few days before the accident, and she didn't seem upset or surprised when Sara lost the baby.

At this point Sara asked, 'Are you saying that we choose our parents?'

'This is an increasingly accepted concept', I answered, 'as we all search for greater meaning in our life, and look to grow to our soul's potential. While this may seem difficult to understand, particularly given some of the seemingly unwise choices that might be made, remember that from a soul's perspective, the contract is to learn, grow, and gain wisdom in each lifetime.

'So didn't my baby's soul think he had made the right choice?' Sara asked.

Trusting in the source of my words, the information flowed effortlessly.

'Exactly the opposite, actually!' I answered, tapping into the wisdom of Krisayah. 'Although it has been very difficult for you since the accident, I sense that your dream visit is meant to help you grow within yourself through understanding why Joseph was only intended to make such a brief visit. There will also have been the needs of Joseph's contract to satisfy for his own soul growth. Naturally, receiving this information can come as a shock. Out of his concern for you, Joseph perhaps felt it wasn't right to maintain the contact in your dream.

'Instead, you were guided to be here today, able to ask your questions and receive his message through me'.

'I have been interested in having some healing since all of this happened', Sara explained. 'I had been given your card on recommendation shortly after the accident. I had totally forgotten about it until I accidentally found it in my wallet the morning after the visit from Joseph!'

'Some people would call that a coincidence!' I answered. 'But in reality there is no such thing. This is just one small example of how you are guided by the universe. Let's explore the significance of Joseph's decision to choose you as his parent. I am not forgetting your husband in all of this; however, for him the reasons may have a different resonance.

'Would you say you are different now than before this happened?' I asked.

'Definitely!' Sara replied. 'I seem to have a greater appreciation about life and what is really important, and because everything can change in an instant, that I should treasure what I have more thoroughly'.

'How has this shown itself?' I asked.

'With this pregnancy, it felt different straight away', Sara answered. 'It was like there was a silver cord of connection between us, right from the moment of conception. When I passed the three-month mark, I thought I was in the clear. I was feeling so happy and healthy, and really looking forward to making our family complete. I now treasure Laura and my husband even more. It seems so unfair that all I did was try to get some fresh air for my baby and myself on a lovely day, and it should end so tragically. But there were lots of witnesses and some of them grabbed the guy who ran into me. Because skateboarding is prohibited in the park and his actions had such an impact on my life, he has been charged and it is going to court very soon'.

'What do you hope to gain by taking him to court?' I needed to ask.

'Justice, of course!' Sara shot back. 'He might have won some recognition for his skateboarding talents in the national championships, but that doesn't mean that he should be allowed to get away with this. He is responsible for me losing my baby'.

'And if he is convicted, how will that help you?' I persisted.

Sara became silent, and then began slowly, showing her huge amount of trust in our exchange. 'I hurt so much in my heart', she confessed. 'We had waited until Laura was about to enter pre-school to have another child so I could focus on the new baby. I am so angry. I guess I want someone to blame, and in this instance, it seems obvious.

'Blame invokes anger, and holds a person in the energy of the event and perpetuates the damage that has happened', I warned. 'It stops your growth on every level. It creates a false view of reality, and therefore every experience and relationship is shadowed in this detrimental and limiting mindset. It is the domain of those who fail to take the opportunity to learn the lesson at hand. In many cases, this means that they are not taking responsibility for the decisions, actions, or events in their own lives.

'Yes, there are instances when someone is at fault, having intentionally set out to cause harm, and they should justifiably be brought to account. However, consider what yourself, your husband, and the skateboarder might learn from this experience. Although you have been through a great deal and it will take time to heal thoroughly, perhaps you could try to step outside of your emotional turmoil and see if there is a greater lesson for you here at this time. This will let the deep healing begin'.

'Are you saying that losing my baby and this dream are part of something greater?' Sara questioned.

'Joseph told you that he was never intended to manifest as your son', I replied. 'Therefore, his contract for this lifetime must have been intended to be fulfilled without the necessity for him to have a physical embodiment on this occasion. His soul will have known when it was time to leave, though it wouldn't necessarily have chosen the circumstances by which to depart. It would just have known its contract was complete and it was time to leave. So, if that is the case, do you think that the skateboarder really was responsible?'

Sara made no reply but needed to ask, 'What would have been his contract for this lifetime?'

'Through exploring his Akashic records – the book of one's many lives – it would be possible to gain some insight. Because it was such a brief visit, I sense that his contract was always intended to be an important one that would benefit all concerned and make a lasting impact on your life, not only for the emotional experience you have undergone, but in other very significant ways yet to be discovered.

'This type of mission is reserved for the more advanced souls, who have relatively few remaining reasons to continually experience being human. These are often the missions of greatest value. For his soul contract, I sense it was an opportunity to reconnect with your soul one final time. You mentioned that there was an easy familiarity between you and an instant connection'.

'It was like I already knew him but couldn't remember where from', Sara said.

'The insight I am receiving tells me that Joseph came to experience the joy of unconditional love through you. In exchange it is most likely that you and Joseph knew each other in at least one previous lifetime', I explained. 'Souls operate in families, and will reconnect with their group in different ways during various lifetimes. You may have been involved with each other in a different relationship than mother and child. Because his contact with you was so caring, I feel that he was acting as a parental figure, trying to guide you and help you grow. This could well be the relationship you once had, during which he was unable to help you as he had intended, either through circumstance or because of choices made by his host at the time. His soul might well have been addressing a final aspect of karma, and by uniting with you once again, he could have been provided the opportunity to release himself, and at the same time help your soul evolve.

> *This type of mission is reserved for the more advanced souls, who have relatively few remaining reasons to continually experience being human.*

'His legacy is to help you grow emotionally, and to help you heal in some way. In this way, it makes him an old soul. You said you sensed his wisdom when you spoke with him in your dream. Just consider for a moment, beyond the recent events and your feelings about them, what important part of your life needs healing?'

Sara sat further back in her chair. She looked like she would have pulled her knees to her chin and wrapped her arms around them to make a shield, had space allowed. It seemed like long time before she replied, 'My relationship with my father'.

'How does this relate to your feelings for him?' I probed.

'I have never forgiven him for leaving us', Sara explained. 'Although I used to miss him terribly, I cannot think of him in a loving way. I was only five. My sister was three, and my mother was pregnant again with twins. My gran said he was too young for all the responsibility. He was only twenty-two when he just didn't come home from work one payday. My mother was heartbroken. They had met at church when she was only fourteen, and married when she was sixteen with her parents blessing. I arrived within that year. He was her first and only love. She dedicated herself to the four of us and never let herself love another man again.

'She was a very caring, good-looking lady, and she worked hard to keep a roof over our heads. She was proud, and always made our birthdays very special. At Christmas she spared no expense, although she would have been saving all year in her little jars and tins. The doctors said she died of a heart attack, which was highly unusual for a woman of only forty-two. But it didn't matter what they said; I knew that she died of a broken heart, and I hate him for it'.

'I understand your situation', I said, 'and this brings further significance to what you have been through. Your lifetime is but a blink of the eye. What you perceive as having happened years ago, in your soul's reality, was merely a nanosecond ago. Remember that your soul has chosen you for the experiences opportunities to grow that your life will offer it. Joseph's soul learning was nearing completion, and this was the time to seize the learning available and thoroughly apply it.

'It is clear that Joseph is definitely directing you to explore your ability to extend forgiveness. Remember that when we are able to look at life from a soul perspective, rather than in terms of human and personal loss and gain, we leave behind the feelings of victimization, unfairness, and bad luck so that we can take spiritual responsibility for what we attract. Then we can truly start to work toward a wonderfully joy-filled and abundant life. We can then begin to understand why and how certain events happen, when we frame them as instruments for our own growth. Consider this: If you were able to forgive the skateboarder how would you feel?'

'I don't know if I am ready for that yet', Sara admitted. 'However, the question does stir some feelings within me'.

'If the act of forgiveness has a deep resonance with you, then there is a good chance that there are deeper layers to be healed', I explained. 'Joseph will have chosen to give this lesson willingly. The ability to honour his decision and to learn and profit from it lies with you, because this will also be part of your soul's journey and growth. Try to put aside your instinctive emotions of right and wrong, blame and guilt, and see the greater benefit to be gained from this event.

'Losing your baby is tragic. However, from a soul perspective, there could be a very different outcome. Imagine two scenes: The first is that you win a conviction against the person who knocked you down, he receives his judgment, and his life is permanently altered. The second is that you drop the charges, become willing to forgive him, and ask him to reflect on his actions. Which do you think would result in greater benefit for all concerned? Have you thought about the likelihood of a champion skateboarder finding himself out of control on a level path? Joseph needed to return to the Kingdom of Souls, and the universe provided the means. This now leaves you with the choice of how to honour your baby's time with you.

'Remember, you do not yet know what other benefits that engaging forgiveness will bring into your life. Once you have learned something, you will no longer attract the same or similar circumstances that brought about the opportunity to learn in the first place. You move on along your path toward wholeness, wisdom, and total happiness'.

At this point, we were obviously getting to the core of the situation.

'And then, if you were able to forgive your father, how would that feel?' I continued. 'You need not answer me now. Take time to sit with these possibilities and see what impact they make'.

'I can make sense of what you are saying', Sara replied, 'but it seems like such a drastic way of getting me to forgive my father'.

'For a soul's existence in each lifetime', I explained, 'it is the mission or contract that is important. We all tend to cloud what might be invaluable learning moments with our humanly emotions, values, and ideas. What would you wish for if you could have anything?'

'If I can't have Joseph, I would like to have my father back in my life again', Sara answered. 'All of this has made me realise how precious life is, and that you should never build regrets out of being stubborn or angry'.

'The journey toward manifesting your wishes lies within your heart', I said, feeling the strong influence of Krisayah. 'Consider the act of forgiveness in its widest applications, and if you are comfortable with invoking this gift of graciousness, you will reap its rewards. Remember that Joseph made this journey for a reason. If learning forgiveness was the gift he was to impart, then you have the opportunity to embrace it now'.

I gave Sara the Soul Forgiveness Intention, which has been successfully used for many clients as well as by myself, and suggested that we meet again in two weeks. In the meantime, I impressed upon her that she should try to establish a daily practice of even just being willing to begin to extend forgiveness. Through doing so, the pain and anger would start to ease, and this would allow her life to move forward.

Two weeks later, Sara returned. As I greeted her at the start of our next session, I couldn't help but notice how much lighter and unburdened she looked. She quickly informed me that after discussing our session with her husband, she had spent some time during the following few evenings reciting the forgiveness mantra and sending forgiveness to the skateboarder, Jason. They had decided to talk to him, and in the company of their solicitors, they had spent two hours going over the events of the incident that had left such a tragic scar. As it turned out, the loss was evident for both parties.

Jason was the only son and main caretaker for his ailing, elderly mother, who had been suffering with terminal cancer, until she had recently been taken into hospital with pneumonia, he had honoured her wishes to care for her in her home. He attended to her needs while maintaining his studies toward a law degree at the nearby university. On the day of the incident, he had received an urgent call from the hospital to say that she had taken a turn for the worse. Living some miles by road from the hospital, he decided in a moment of panic-influenced reasoning to cut through the park on his skateboard. He knew it was illegal, but he was willing to take the gamble, given the circumstances.

With the paths so busy with pedestrians, he was growing increasingly frustrated and anxious about making it to the hospital. His angst gave way to floods of uncontrollable tears, which is why he literally didn't see Sara. He was simply in a blind panic. When the witnesses grabbed hold of him to restrain him, they thought his struggles were an attempt to escape his wrong doing and held him more firmly. The onlookers who described the look of anger and rage on his face misinterpreted his anguish in knowing his mother was dying only half a mile away.

Because of this incident, he arrived at the hospital too late. His solicitor confirmed his mother's passing. Later, upon learning what had happened to Sara, his grief was compounded by sorrow regarding the loss he had caused Sara and her husband. He could only apologise from the depths of his heart, knowing that this was inadequate.

Since the meeting, her and her husband had discussed at length their growing sense of acceptance and understanding concerning Jason's situation. They had decided to drop the charges.

This now left her free to start to heal on this level, and she continued her progress by envisioning extending forgiveness to her father, along with the intention that they should be reunited. This had been difficult, but she had found that sitting quietly while holding a photograph of him allowed her to connect with him more easily. Now, her feelings were more geared towards wanting to find him and get to know him. Sadly, she had no clues regarding his whereabouts.

SOUL WHISPERING

What we think about most, we attract to ourselves.

$\mathcal{I}$ encouraged Sara to continue to spend a few minutes each day with her father's photo, and to send welcoming, loving, and forgiving thoughts to him. Beyond that, she was to trust in the universe to hear her soul's request. I guided her to focus on the vision of being reunited with her father, rather than 'how' this might come about. Just know, I advised, that if it is meant to be, it will happen.

Sara's willingness to look beyond her personal tragedy enabled a major shift to happen in her soul's journey. She provided this example for her husband, and he, in turn, benefited. Sara left our second meeting, saying that she intended to plant a beautiful flowering bush, which was known to attract numerous butterflies, in their garden as a living memorial and reminder of Joseph.

I informed Sara that she had intuitively chosen wisely, because butterflies are the symbol of transformation. What could be more appropriate?

CHAPTER 8

Love — Your Soul's Greatest Quest

CHAPTER 8

Love — Your Soul's Greatest Quest

With love, anything is possible. Start with your dreams.

*I*f we acknowledge that, essentially, we are all capable of love, and that this fundamental emotion should be the most nurturing, comforting, healing, and supportive of anything we experience in our lives, then why is it also the one that brings the most pain, self destruction, and challenge at times?

SOUL WHISPERING

The language of your heart is universal.
Listen to your heart and be as your soul.

*L*ove is the most consistently sought-out emotion by each and every human being, from one life to the next through the guidance of the soul. This is a testament to its power and durability. It is a clue as to the most important factor for our own human development and our soul's growth. It may be why the soul chooses to return again and again, so that it can experience a greater variety of growth opportunities. It is the most powerful and provocative emotion known to man, and yet it is also the most misunderstood, misrepresented, misused, abused, and unappreciated quality we embody.

Giving and receiving genuine love comes through a deep sense of self-knowing and acceptance. It is true that if we love ourselves, we are able to extend love without expectation to another, when we choose to, because we are not looking for someone else to somehow know what it is that we need to make us feel complete. So often, though, we leave out the part about getting to know, accept, and love ourselves, and go straight to trying to attract someone in order to prove ourselves lovable. This backward approach often leads to numerous failed relationships, and patterns of behaviour that do not serve us, or bring any positive good or growth.

Your soul's message: I ask you to invest in yourself by taking some time to get to know yourself, smooth your rough edges, heal your wounds, and release expectancy of others. By generating self-acceptance and self-love, you open the gateway to experiencing the most wonderful state of being.

We are force fed images from a very early age about the fantasy of finding our one true love, although reality shows us that it is a rarity for someone to progress through an entire life with the same companion. There almost seems to be an unseen pressure that urges us to couple up as soon as possible. This means that a young person just starting out on the relationship rollercoaster has most likely not explored their own self-love and personal value, or set their boundaries regarding acceptable behaviour from a partner, and in many cases themselves. They fervently seek a partner (or several) to either replace what they see happening with their parents or to compensate for it. In reality, it is a frightening truth that many people are not taught how to love themselves in a nurturing, respectful way that would make the foundations for true love in later life so much more possible. This is not anyone's fault. One cannot teach what they have not been taught or experienced for themselves. However, we live in an age where there is an increasing chance of self-love appreciation being part of a good, balanced upbringing.

For those without a good example to follow, this sets up a pattern as they move from one relationship to another. With each new one, they try to find what the last one didn't offer. At the same time, as the number of failed relationships grows, there is more to heal and repair, and thus the expectancy on the new partner increases. This is a recipe for a lifetime of feeling unfulfilled and, ultimately, unlovable. This means that, should a genuinely loving, warm, and balanced partner present themselves, these kinds of people are too scared and skeptical to recognise it.

SOUL WHISPERING

We attract that which mirrors our inner beliefs about ourselves. Be sure to radiate your most positive qualities, as this will act as a beam and draw those who genuinely recognise these higher qualities in themselves.

*D*ifferent partners bring a variety of gifts and growth opportunities, since they too are developing along the spectrum. It is almost inevitable that we are going to encounter challenges within our relationships. These are reflections of our own inner challenges. What we must remember is that we attract our partners as a manifestation of our opinion of ourselves. We can only recognise in others what is already within us. We cannot hope to find the 'perfect' partner because we are not 'perfect' ourselves.

It is said that our personality, views, behaviour, and beliefs are formed from a blend of the characters, strengths, and weaknesses of the five people we spend the most time with! How does that apply to you? Equally, if we want to get a good picture of what we are like and how others see us, we need only take a look at those five people from that perspective.

Where are you in the relationship stakes at present? Are you reluctantly single, blissfully single, regrettably in a relationship and wanting out, or deliriously attached and loving every minute? What follows is intended to act as a service to your soul when it comes to relationships.

First of all, single or not, you are your own person. You were born an individual, with a soul on a mission, a life to lead, and experiences to have. You have every right to be loved, secure, and happy. There is no other person who can make you complete other than yourself. Because your soul is wise and richly endowed, you already have within you everything you need to make your life one of joy, contentment, and abundance. It is the external pressures, often brought on by comparing ourselves to others around us, that make us think we are incomplete, worthless, undesirable, too old, too large, not wealthy enough, and so on. We often inadvertently adopt these false beliefs as our measure of our lovability, desirability, and worthiness. It is possible to change from being reluctantly single and looking for a partner without success to being blissfully single, and from there, when you are ready for a relationship, to finding the right person! Here's how:

Remember that what you radiate returns to you magnified. If you send out an energy message from a mindset of desperation that says, 'I am looking for someone, anyone, to love and to love me. I am a nice person. Won't somebody love me, please', you will attract a person who senses your desperation because they can 'read' your message, since they have the same feelings. This is not the type of foundation on which a solid, loving, balanced, and caring relationship can grow. Both parties will be needy, each expecting the other to make everything all right. They are entering into the relationship from a point of weakness, looking for 'what can I gain from this', rather than a strong belief in themselves, with the offer, 'this is what I have an abundance of to share with you'.

Expectancy – the self-generated but unspoken ideas about how you want your partner to behave – leads to a huge percentage of all arguments and tension within relationships. Somehow we think that our partner 'should know' what we are thinking, or what should be done to make us happy, even if it is taking out the garbage without being asked.

When you notice this happening, recognise that expectancy is an uninformed attempt to communicate through your psychic ability. Before that can happen, each person must be willingly on the same wavelength, tuned-in, and working in harmony. For this to be possible, one must be able into tune one's intuition or soul's voice first, before expecting another to respond favourably. If both partners are collaborating intuitively, then the expectancy and the mild manipulation and frustration that go with it dissolve. What most of us experience, though, is regular disappointment when, yet again, our inner wishes and hopes are not recognised. This can change with conscious attention and good communication between the partners.

To transform yourself into a more intriguing, blissfully single person, you would benefit from initially getting to know and love yourself. Explore your values, and the lessons you've learned so far, and make sure that you feed yourself properly, get enough sleep, and drink plenty of fresh water. Look at your wardrobe, and choose the colours and styles that say: 'I am comfortable with myself; I open myself to all good experiences'. Give yourself some treats that show you appreciate yourself and that your hard-earned money is not just to pay bills and other obligations. Then, when you are 'in the groove', take a look in the mirror and say to yourself several times, 'I am whole and complete just as I am. I love myself, therefore I am loveable'. It will feel uncomfortable at first, and there may even be a few tears! But keep at it, every morning for twenty-eight days! If you repeat an action or set of words eight times or more in succession, a new neural pathway is created in the brain, which means that new hardwiring has taken place. So, it won't take long before you begin making decisions about life, opportunities, new friendships and possible relationships that reflect this new level of self-belief and self-love.

I have noticed that subtle but significant changes are taking place within me when my handwriting changes and takes on a different style, when my signature changes, or when I start to wear different colours. I take these as signs that a shift is happening deep within my soul, and that it will make its way to my consciousness in a short while. And it always does, bringing with it the courage, energy, or creativity to take my life to that next stage. Another transformative indicator, especially for women, is to suddenly have a completely new hairstyle! Others may feel drawn to express their budding growth by having something more permanent like a tattoo or body piercing. These are expressions from deep within that try to convey the message of the true self at that time.

Another exercise is to take some time with pen and paper and write down the qualities you find most attractive or desirable in your close friends and family. Now ask yourself how you display these qualities. You can only see in others that which you already have within yourself. Thinking of the same, or perhaps a larger group of people, repeat the exercise, but this time think about the things that annoy or irritate you, and again see how these reflect in you. Next, focus on how you could highlight the positive elements and diminish the negative ones. Conclude this exercise by writing the following statement, while repeating it aloud several times: 'My life and relationships allow me to authentically be myself and reflect my most positive attributes. I am whole and complete. I am content. And so it is'.

Being 'blissfully single' is a tremendously empowering and attractive energy state to embrace. If you are radiating this, you naturally look and feel great! Your confidence levels are high, and you are self-assured and focused on how good life can be. Yes, there may be lonely days; however, you are moving forward and not looking back. When you are in this energy state, it is more likely that you will attract people who feel the same way about themselves. Being in the mindset that you have newly created means that you will not jump at the chance for a relationship simply because someone is better than no one! You will feel that you have a great deal more to offer that special person, and therefore, because the state of being 'blissfully single' is so comfortable, you will relinquish this status only when the right person arrives in your life.

If you are in a relationship that is tired and past its best, try the writing exercise above with the aim of reconnecting yourself with what initially attracted you to your partner and what you hoped to bring to the relationship. You might even do the exercise with your partner, as this would remind both, and make you aware of the areas that have mellowed since you have been together. Obviously, events during a relationship can determine its direction and strength, and this must be taken into consideration. However, if the pair of you truly want to make it work, sit down and look at the challenges you have faced and discuss what you have learned individually and as a couple from each event. Look at the positives; there will always be some, even if they are hidden beneath emotional baggage. Then, build on these gifts. Having acknowledged the learning, start to move forward stronger and more united, because shared events serve to knit people together in unique ways that could not be imagined. Your souls will already be in communication and will only want what is in the highest good for each of you.

Events during a relationship can determine its direction and strength

If you are a member of the deliriously attached brigade, then help yourself maintain this and make your relationship even stronger by listing all the things that you are grateful for. Be specific. Don't just think of material possessions; include the emotional, psychological, and spiritual benefits such as trust, fidelity, reliability, unconditional love, freedom to express your authentic self, and so on, which are the bedrock of your relationship. Giving thanks and extending gratitude ensures that more wonderfulness comes your way and that you do not loose what you already have.

I am so often asked about relationship issues. One of the most common concerns is that the choices one makes repeatedly result in attracting the same 'type' of person. This means that my clients find that their relationships follow a predictable pattern, and when each ends, it adds to the burden of 'failed' attempts to find lasting love. My guidance here asks them to employ the techniques outlined above, namely, learning to love yourself and be kind to yourself. Know that you are loveable. Acquaint yourself with your best character attributes, and work to release the less desirable ones. Explore what it is that you hope a relationship can bring you. Be totally honest with yourself, because whatever you expect a partner to bring is exactly what you need to build within yourself before you can attract the right person.

Look at the patterns in your life, and what attracts you to the same type of person each time, because this is a mirror of yourself, your areas of required growth, and perhaps where healing is needed. Once you have recognised what it is you are reflecting, address the issues within yourself and work towards being 'blissfully single'. Then, maintain your inner belief in being able to attract someone who reflects the soul-empowered you!

So often, we allow ourselves to be blind to the reality within our relationships, yet deep inside, our soul knows that in order to fix what's wrong, we need to heal ourselves first. We do this because we think it is easier and kinder to maintain the status quo. In reality, this is not the way to run a relationship, because nobody is growing or being true to their soul's needs. We let events unfold that will determine the direction or longevity of the relationship, and breathe a sigh of relief when we are released from its ties without having to do the hard work of ending it ourselves. Inevitably, when we learn to listen to our soul and how it talks to us through our health and our experiences, we have the responsibility to honour these messages and act upon them. Otherwise, we may find ourselves experiencing avoidable stress, challenge, and hardship.

SOUL WHISPERING

When something or someone challenges you, you are being given an opportunity to grow. Seize it, and embrace the lesson, and this will soon let other opportunities follow.

*M*y client Susan's case highlights one example of this concept. At age thirty-five, she found herself at a turning point in her life. Her story is not uncommon. Her sister, who was concerned about the changes she had witnessed in her, recommended her to me. What turned out to be our only session began with me saying, 'Tell me what you are seeking and how I may help.

'I am feeling so lost and rejected and unworthy since my relationship ended', Susan confided. 'I need to move forward, but I have no emotional strength or direction'.

'What has lead you to this point in your life?' I asked.

'Six months ago', Susan explained, 'my boyfriend, Charles, and I had a huge argument, and after a fiery, four-year relationship, we split up. He has been calling me lately, and has invited me to a concert next weekend to see one of my favourite bands. He knows how much I want to go, so I guess he feels fairly confident that I will say yes. I am not sure what to do because of what has gone on in the past. I told Jenna, my sister, that I was considering going with him, and she was so angry with me that she didn't speak to me for a day! She was the one who listened and supported me through the last four years.

'He is five years older than me. He lives over three hours away, so we only used to see each other at weekends and when we could arrange a holiday. When we met, I had been looking for a partner for a long time, and I was relieved when he was interested in me. I thought I had found my soul mate. Our birthdays are close together, so we have the same star sign, and we seemed to have lots in common.

'He was charming, romantic, loved to travel, and was always surprising me with gifts, expensive meals, and poetry he had written that spoke of his love. I guess he knew what would win my heart. I must admit that I was totally besotted and fell in love with him very quickly, even though Jenna and my friends didn't like him much.

'When we were together, it was always exciting, although he was a thrill seeker and his driving used to terrify me! I had been bored in my previous relationship, and he was so different to my previous boyfriend. His parents were lovely and welcomed me into the family straight away. We spoke at least five times each day, and once, after we had a little spat, because he wouldn't answer his phone, I drove to his house that evening to see him, just to apologise, and then drove back again. I was a bit disappointed when he was less pleased to see me than I expected, but we moved on from there and everything was okay for a while.

'I am very aware that the honeymoon period of any relationship should not be taken as reality. However, with not seeing each other every day, when we would meet up, I always felt the thrill of anticipation like on a first date! I often felt like I was falling in love with him again each time we met. We shared some great times together.

'He was very possessive right from the start, and I initially took this as a sign of his feelings, because he said he missed me and would rather be by my side. I am, or should I say was, a naturally outgoing, independent, and spontaneous person, so if perhaps I had decided to visit a friend or go shopping without telling him, and I wasn't at home when he rang, he would sulk and imply that I was cheating on him.

'No matter how hard I tried to convince him of the innocent truth, he would persist until we would have a big argument and not speak for a few days, and then one of us would do something to break the silence. I was blinded by my love and presumed that the blame was all mine. My friends saw the changes in me over time and said that he was a controlling emotional and mental bully, but I didn't listen. I know this makes me sound so tremendously naïve, but it was like I was under a spell or something'.

SOUL WHISPERING

Because we are all souls that are here on Earth to learn, do not be too hard on yourself. Life can be challenging enough on its own without adding to it with self-criticism.

*L*ast year', Susan continued, 'he unexpectedly lost his job. I was not convinced by the reasons he gave for this. I suspected that it was over something to do with his behaviour at work with one of the girls in the office; he liked to have the attention of the women all the time. However, he found other employment within a few months.

'During this period, I am pretty certain that he had a fling while he was out on a stag night. His friends were unusually nervous when we met up with them the following weekend, and I overheard one of them comment on his behaviour. He acted strange and distant for a couple of weeks, but after I paid him loads of attention, he finally came round again. He denied that anything had happened, of course, but this rocked me to the core. I just felt numb, rejected, and betrayed. It lowered my self-esteem and self-confidence even more, and yet I tried harder and harder to hang on to him. I felt as though he was my reason for living, and if he didn't want me, then my life was meaningless.

'When I got promoted, my salary increased dramatically and he no longer earned as much as me. We talked about this on numerous occasions. It didn't bother me in particular, because when we met I was just starting new career and didn't have any spare money for a while. Because he had a good, well-salaried job at the time, he paid for the lion's share of things, as he said he wasn't concerned about money in that way. I thought he was so generous, but always tried to contribute in one way or another, and don't feel I ever took it for granted. Before we split, he had begun to expect me to pay for everything. I never asked him to contribute – I didn't dare – but he was more than capable of paying his share, or offering, at least.

'We split up a couple of times, but we always got back together. When we finished this last time, I thought it was for good. I had sensed for a while that he was losing interest and getting bored. We were like an old married couple. I tried to suggest that we take regular weekends away, and mentioned that, perhaps, if I could get a transfer to his town, we could live together, but he showed little desire to spend time with me, let alone create a home together.

'With everything that had gone on, my self-esteem was so low that I found myself constantly feeling that everything was my fault, which meant that I was always apologising for everything that happened, even if it had nothing to do with me. I felt I shouldn't have an opinion, and that I should take the blame for anything that went even slightly wrong. With all this regular stress, I put on a lot of weight and stopped taking care of myself, which he said was why we hadn't had a good physical relationship for ages. Yet in the beginning, when I dressed nicely, did my hair, and put on make-up, he would constantly nag me about trying to attract other blokes, even though I was making an effort to look nice for him. D'you know, I am hearing myself say this and I must sound totally crazy. Why didn't I see what was going on? Even after all this, I still miss him. Now I am torn in two between what my heart and my head are telling me'.

SOUL WHISPERING

*When we look outside ourselves for love and
validation of who we are, we silence our own
ability to love ourselves unconditionally.
Therefore, we allow others to control how we
feel about ourselves, which can only ever be a
reflection of how they feel about themselves.*

*S*usan was near to tears at this point, and she needed a few
moments to compose herself. When she was ready, the session
continued. She seemed to have so much to convey, yet it all focused
around one central theme.

When she was finished, she sat back in her chair. My connection
with the underlying messages felt like a dam about to burst.

'I would like to help you understand the meaning of this
relationship', I began. 'My role as a Soul Whisperer is to act as a
coach and guide, extend healing, and inspire those who are ready to
work with the messages from their soul. What we put out, we attract
back. This works on every level, and for some the words may seem
harsh. However, it is not my intention to assign blame or impose
guilt.

'The underlying thread that ties everything you have told me
together is that, although you may not realise it just yet, you have
been given an amazing chance to grow, define yourself, and cleanse
your life through meeting Charles. You mentioned that you felt he
was your soul mate. So often, we think of this as being someone with
whom we share the most amazing, lovingly intimate relationship.
In truth, a soul mate is someone whose soul has vowed to take on a
certain role and has set up a contract with your soul for that purpose.

When this individual arrives in your life, you may feel very quickly that you have a deep connection, and yet their purpose is to help you grow – to move you significantly forward along your spiritual path. They may or may not strike a romantic chord within your heart. This is not essential for the role they play and their value in your life.

'Some soul mates may be your greatest adversaries, and yet without their presence and challenges, you might not develop to your full potential. Someone may be in your life temporarily, as part of their soul's contract of growth. So, I would agree that Charles probably was a soul mate, just not in the sense that you are thinking.

'Remember, we can have many soul mates in our lifetime. Not all are going to be the opposite sex, or romantically linked to us, but one thing is certain: they will all help us grow in some positive way or another before they move on. The secret is to recognise the learning that they offer us so that we do not have to repeat the lessons again. A soul mate that stays with you in a loving relationship for a lifetime may have made a vow in a previous life to take on this role.

Someone may be in your life temporarily, as part of their soul's contract of growth.

'Consider also that whether someone is your soul mate or not, the very fact that their soul has chosen another life here on the earthly school for souls means that they, too, have learning to achieve, and for that reason, each of us participates in the growth of others, knowingly or not.

'For some, it could be that they need plenty of reassurance and attention. Their way of getting this is by being exaggerated in their behaviour and demonstrations of affection. This is the pattern of someone who feels inadequate or lacks self-confidence. If this type of person seems to get bored after a while, it will be because everything became too familiar. There was no more challenge, and as you said yourself, you lost your sparkle, which would have been the very thing that attracted him to you in the first place.

'Initially, your confidence and strength will have been desirable, and a challenge to engage with. However, as time progressed, this turned into a threat because underneath you are a very strong person, and it shows against a weaker character.

'All of this maintains this type of person's position of control and power, but it does not nurture growth. It is sometimes the only way someone like this can express themselves, and yet, if they could connect with their inner truth, they would be able to relax their behaviour and realise that they can both give and receive love without the need for dramatic highlights.

'The gifts, holidays, and high living seem, in this case, to be all material, external compensations for a lack of internal spiritual wealth and integrity. His soul's learning needs are speaking to him through his actions. This translates into the kind of behaviour you have experienced. In order to help you move forward, consider the following:

'What we find attractive in others reflects the characteristics we like about ourselves. Equally, what annoys or upsets us reflects what we recognize about our behaviour or ourselves that sits uncomfortably with us. Naturally, in most cases, similar personalities attract each other. However, when a bit of time passes, it is unlikely for two equally strong individuals to be able to form a lasting bond without one of them becoming weaker.

'What attracted Charles to you initially started to become a challenge when you gained confidence and confronted his behaviour. The distance between you and the frequency of your time together meant that this took longer to become evident.

'You have no need to feel numb, rejected, or betrayed because you have a choice about adopting any or all of these states of consciousness. Numbness is a form of protection, and it is a natural response when you feel you have exposed yourself emotionally. Rejection and betrayal, however, are two of the most damaging events to happen to any person. It is a strong soul who chooses these lessons. In other words, you can feel hurt and stay wounded as deeply and for as long as you choose. You have the strength to explore the learning that is being offered to you and to use this to benefit your soul and your future.

'Once you have mastered these lessons, you do not have to repeat them, which means that this could well lead you to the most amazing, genuinely loving relationship you could ever imagine. Remember that you host a soul that chose you and the life your spirit would lead when it contracted to experience certain opportunities to grow and learn more about the art of being human. Your soul chose a host who had a strong sense of self, who believed in the possibility of finding true love, and who was dedicated to trying to maintain this ideal.

'Without realising it, the fact that you are questioning whether to go to the concert shows that you have successfully accomplished this important opportunity for growth. In a way, you have provided Charles with an opportunity for his own soul to grow, if he chooses to acknowledge the lesson. However, as the pleasure and peril of the human species, it is free will that determines our choices, and thus our progress, and the soul will respond accordingly.

'Finally, when you say you are torn between your heart and your head, what you are actually feeling is probably the fear of missing out on what you remember as the good bits of the relationship. Sit quietly with yourself and ask, 'If I were to act in accordance with my soul, what would my decision be?' When you listen with your heart, you will always receive the guidance that is in your best interest, because you are connected with the energy of self-love. Sometimes, we may mentally argue with ourselves because our consciousness is trying to convince us otherwise. However, it is the truth of the soul that speaks louder and clearer using the language of unconditional love. The soul does not argue! You will carry forth with you from this day the advantage of wisdom as your mentor. Your true heart would never guide you to be hurt in any way.

Susan had sat perfectly still during this transmission. What remained was the question of whether she should accept Charles' invitation to the concert.

'Having heard what your soul has to say, does this make your decision about going to the concert any clearer?' I asked.

She paused for quite a while, as though she was asking herself the question she had just been guided to explore.

'I have been through so much in the last few years', she finally responded. 'I have lost myself and had to fight to find the real me again. After over a year of not tending to my hair, Jenna finally nagged me into making an appointment, and I gave my hairdresser free reign to style it. Her words, when she was finished, reduced me to tears, when she gave me the mirror and said, 'Welcome back!'

'I don't know if this is relevant, but just as I was starting to feel a glimmer of the 'old me' starting to rekindle last month, I took myself away to a spa retreat for two weeks. During my absence, my home was all but destroyed when the flat roof of my two-storey penthouse apartment collapsed under the weight of last month's ten days of heavy rain. Because I was away when it happened, the damage went undetected until the rainwater seeped through to the apartment below mine! I have been living with Jenna while the repairs are being done.

'The police eventually had to break in, and were up to their calves in accumulated water as they walked through the living room, dining room, and kitchen. When they went upstairs, there was a huge hole in the ceiling of my spacious bedroom that opened to the sky where the roof should have been! Almost of all my personal things, and most of the furniture I had saved for over the years, cannot be repaired and are, by now, in a landfill somewhere.

'By the time I was allowed access, I had lost most of my clothes and any fabric or paper things because they were covered in mould and had started to rot. All the letters, cards, and poetry he wrote, as well as the photographs, gifts, and the teddy bear he bought me for our first Valentine's Day are all gone. It was as though my precious home, which I had spent ages making my sanctuary, was crying with me over all of this.

'Your home both nurtures you and takes on your energy', I said. 'It reflects how you feel about yourself and what you are going through. In return, it can energetically support you, help you to heal and build solid foundations that will benefit every day of your life. Your bedroom is especially attuned to your energy, the quality of your relationships, and your level of self-love.

'When it is rebuilt', Susan explained, 'I will have a completely new interior – wiring, plumbing, carpets, kitchen, bathroom, and everything! I have even asked for some of the walls to be moved to make it more spacious! I am getting the chance to design my home exactly how I want it! Now that it is starting to take shape, I am coming to terms with what I have lost, and I am trying to enjoy creating my sanctuary, though I do find it very stressful. Jenna has been fantastic, and I am very lucky to have her for my sister. However, I am so looking forward to being back in my own space. I just can't understand my luck!'

'Water is the great emotional cleanser', I explained, 'and it may be that this incident is the universe's way of clearing out the old hurts, negativity, and pain with respect to this relationship. We measure the impact of such events at the level of human emotion, on a "how-does-this-affect-me" scale, and the various levels of cost we perceive. If you emotionally remove yourself from the equation and operate at your soul level, then perhaps you might find the blessing in this event. You are being given a totally fresh start, and although it is stressful now, you will ultimately be stronger and move forward from this situation. If you were not living with Jenna, you perhaps would not be with me today! Everything has its reason, its season, and its time'.

'Taking the time at the retreat was my initial attempt to make a fresh start', Susan said. 'Apparently my treasured home had the same idea! So no, while I did still have a faint yearning in my heart for Charles, I realise that it is the excitement and companionship I miss. So, it is my soul that I am going to listen to. I now have to gather the lessons and make good of them. To go to the concert would only be going backwards, and I do not intend to go back there ever again. Thank you'.

There was no need to thank me, and I instead suggested that she thank her soul and congratulate herself for honouring her new wisdom.

When we evaluate our relationships and feel there are changes that would benefit them, we should start by looking at what it is we would like to change about ourselves. Often, without creating expectancy around your partner, if we adjust our own energy, the union will automatically come into alignment and move forward in its most soul nourishing way for both parties. Looking to others to make things right is not the way to bring about lasting change.

Above all, keep your relationship with yourself honest, authentic, consistent, and filled with integrity and unconditional love. This will ensure that you radiate the best possible tractor beam, should you wish to share your time with someone.

CHAPTER 9

Discover Your Soul's Purpose

CHAPTER 9

Discover Your Soul's Purpose

*When you are in harmony with your soul, you awaken within
you the world of infinite possibilities that is your birthright.*

*D*iscovering your soul's purpose is not a 'one-size-fits-all'
experience. It is not homogenised into categories or filtered into neat
strategies like a corporate mission statement.

Your soul purpose is uniquely about you. It is achieved through
a lifetime's synergy between your soul, your spirit, and your higher
self. Outwardly, some may find themselves hosting the same 'calling',
however, the internal experience will exclusively belong to each
person.

Your soul's purpose is the expression of the contract your soul
created before it chose you as its host for this lifetime. Souls journey
through many hundreds – if not thousands – of lifetimes to gain
understanding, knowledge, and appreciation of the human condition.
From the soul's perspective, this is its very reason for being here in
this host body at this time. For the host – that's you – the collective

lessons the soul has gathered through its many lifetimes bring you the potential of great satisfaction, enjoyment, fulfillment, and a sense of enrichment, which can only be described as all encompassing.

Connecting with your soul's purpose can be intentionally directed through meditation, contemplation, or visualisation. Many people simply commit themselves to following their intuition, in the sure and certain knowledge that they will make the right choices and meet the right people at the most opportune time to allow them to naturally progress toward the reality of meeting their life's purpose. A significant majority stumble blindly through life, waiting naively for their life to reward them simply for their presence.

SOUL WHISPERING

The tools to carve the life you were meant to live are always in reach. Take time to learn how to use them skillfully, and your reward will be a masterpiece.

*Y*ou will recognise the presence of your soul's purpose and even when you are on the path to fulfilling it, because your heart energy will start to sing. You will find yourself literally lost in your own world, providing your own backing track and secretly wishing that nothing would ever change. When you ultimately manifest your soul's intention, you will find that life's challenges become secondary to the deep inner knowledge that you are in the right place, doing what you are meant to do.

This does not mean that your world is necessarily sugar coated or diamond encrusted. Far from it! Living a life where your soul's purpose is being played out may involve taking risks, facing challenges, and responding to difficult situations. Your soul's purpose is all about learning and inner growth, which is achieved through the route most suited to your personality, circumstances, and willingness to explore your full potential.

Honour your calling and embrace it full.

Your soul's message: Honour your calling and embrace it fully, because it is through this that you will experience the greatest rewards.

When you define and connect with your soul's intention, you uncover a direction that will guide your life. This form of anchor can be very reassuring; it allows you to focus your energy and efforts with a meaningful objective. Many find this the thread that weaves many previous experiences together, giving them meaning.

When an individual makes this connection, their heart is enveloped with a deep sense of peace and serenity. Usually, this can be witnessed in the effortless manner with which they deal with difficulties or challenges. Often accompanied by few words and a soft, gentle smile, the soul-actualized person seems to hover over the circumstances presented to them, and glide unflustered towards a solution, no matter what. They are centred, healthy, and willing to continue to learn from others on every level.

With this awareness, decisions are made easier, opportunities are attracted and recognised for their formative influence, the right people appear and bring their contributions for all to benefit, and life carries a quality of divine meaningfulness. With this sense of purpose, obstacles are easily dissolved, and challenges are viewed as opportunities for growth and a demonstration of resourcefulness.

One's soul purpose may have many stages or layers to be explored and satisfied. A soul contract may involve a variety of lessons, experiences, and influences that will help the soul progress along its path. Satisfying one stage will naturally open up the next. The saying, 'You are only given the amount of challenge you can cope with', reflects this reality. For some, life may seem to be a continual series of challenges. While it is important to remember that we attract our reality, we also have a reason for being here. Using the foundation of the soul's purpose as the platform upon which all life experiences can build, we can then employ the universal laws to their fullest effect.

SOUL WHISPERING

Trust as you progress. You are always supported, guided, and cared for unconditionally.

$\mathcal{I}$t is often the domain of the younger souls to learn and explore the simpler attributes of being human. This does not mean that only children or young people host these souls. What it does mean is that these people, as their years unfold, experience life's events without the resourcefulness or general common sense or innate knowledge that others posses. Everything is fresh and new, and at times they seem to lack inner wisdom.

They may learn quickly from each challenge. However, because their judgment is somewhat undeveloped, they may fall prey to the powerful influences of excessive alcohol and drug abuse, perhaps to mimic a perpetual daydream, or return to the memory of the more carefree state of their time as a disembodied soul. The more intermediate journeying soul may repeat patterns in relationships, or become entangled in the continually unsatisfied quest for material rewards and ego-driven behaviour. They know that there is something better to be had from life, but instead of looking inwardly for guidance and clarification, they search outwardly, all the time ignoring the sage within.

The advanced soul houses a stillness and wise quietness that may often be misinterpreted as detachment or disinterest. In reality, they have seen it all before, and are here to experience their few remaining lessons before they are able to elevate their role and serve a greater spectrum of humanity. They can choose to deliver this service either by working on the earthly plane in the human form, or – after they leave their most recent host – by working in one of the higher dimensions of existence.

There are many old souls reincarnating at this time, and steadily over the last two or three decades they have been bringing with them amazing amounts of collected wisdom. They are so familiar with the schooling system that they find it boring and unessential, as they have learned from their many previous lifetimes what is 'really' important to understand and know in order to move forward. These wise ones have been given the names of Indigo, Crystal, Rainbow, or Star children.

These terms reflect their advanced spiritual maturity, their auric luminescence, and their universal connections, which remain strong throughout their life. They are often the children who display heightened psychic talents and despite formal schooling, they retain an unerring wealth of inner knowing and connection. Often labeled difficult to teach, having a low attention span, they are highly aware, although perhaps not able to articulate it in their younger years, of their role and responsibility to be instrumental in taking humanity forward in their lifetime. In their adolescence, they may not conform, expressing their individual uniqueness, and yet they have a strong appreciation for personal growth, the healing arts, and following a career that is creative and satisfying, rather than simply working for the money at the end of the month.

In some cases, they nearly seem to 'have it all' – academic success and social popularity reinforced by strong self-respect and self-worth. Many excel at sports, dancing, or acting – basically anything where they can be physically expressive and share this with an audience. They are often quite artistic in some form, and it is through their chosen medium that they touch others deep within in order to convey their special messages. They often have loving parents who support them during their growth and maturing years with sound guidance that acknowledges their advanced knowledge. Their trouble-free lives are almost like their soul is enjoying a holiday before the full scope of their reason for being called to Earth at this time is put into action. When that time comes, they are refreshed and ready for the fullness of their soul contract to unfold, and they greet this challenge with maturity, willingness, and wisdom.

As adults, whom many of them are now becoming, they are often healers, writers, spiritual teachers, philosophers, and visionaries, sharing their lifetimes of accumulated knowledge, insight, and understanding about the art of being human within their chosen communities. As is becoming more common, this is happening through the multi-media of spiritually oriented films, personal growth programmes, books, DVDs, and the Internet to a hungry audience seeking direction and guidance. This is like a wave of the gentlest perfumed breeze, which is welcome and refreshing at the same time, yet it blows constantly and therefore carves a new landscape through its persistence.

Whatever the 'entry point' of a soul as it chooses and connects with its host, the intention is that it will learn through the experiences provided by the spirit, personality, and choices made during its lifetime. It will make progress as a demonstration of this learning, and then, when it is time to rejoin its soul family, it will take with it valuable wisdom that will be reviewed and added to the collective, universal body of knowledge, and assimilated in order for the next hosting contract to be determined, based on the subsequent stages of knowledge to be gained.

When the soul is not following its intended purpose, the host will find himself experiencing a myriad of challenging realities. These may range from a deep sense of feeling lost and detached from the world around them, to experiencing repeated negative experiences because the lessons being offered are not being appreciated, to constant feelings of frustration, limitation, and thwarted attempts to make good come of their current situation.

SOUL WHISPERING

When you find yourself drawn to something that is out of the normal range of your interests or habits, take note, because the universe won't let an opportunity go by you if it is meant for you. Take action the first time you get the nudge and follow your instincts.

*C*onnecting with your soul's purpose can be done in many ways. At the core of this experience is a willingness to ask, and then listen to the soul once a connection has been made. This is a relatively simple process that requires only some quiet time alone, and the chance to ask the right questions.

SOUL PURPOSE CONNECTION

*T*ake some time away from disruptive noises, with the telephone turned off, and perhaps some gentle instrumental music playing softly in the background, and ensure that you will not be disturbed for about twenty minutes.

Sitting comfortably – not lying down – focus on your breathing. Become aware of your feet, and progressively relax each part of your body one section at a time, as you work toward your head and neck. If your mind starts to chatter and nag you, simply thank it for its awareness and tell it to wait its turn for proper recognition.

Now, keeping your breathing deep and slow, imagine a beam of luminescent white light coming down from the skies above your head, through the top of your head where your Crown Chakra is located.

Progressing slowly, this diamond-like white light then passes down to the centre of your brow to the Third Eye Chakra, where it takes on a beautiful purple-blue indigo hue. Take a few deep breaths.

From there, it descends to the deep blue domain of the communication centre of the Throat Chakra. Breathe deeply again.

After resting here for a few moments, it then continues to the centre of the chest to the seat of compassion and forgiveness known as the Higher Heart Chakra, where the light beam has now become a soft, velvety pink.

Finally, still breathing slowly and deeply, visualise the energy source reaching the Heart Chakra, the resting place of the soul energy evident between each heartbeat. The colour is now a verdant luminosity.

Focus once again on your breathing, as you raise your hands in the prayer position to the Heart centre at the breastbone level. Pause as you slowly repeat these words: 'I welcome my soul's presence. I honour my soul's intentions. I am willing to connect with my soul's purpose'.

Now, from your Third Eye Chakra, imagine a beam of pure indigo light extending from this energy centre to the chamber created by your upheld hands. Direct your awareness, using your senses, to the hollow between your hands. What do you sense?

When you are ready, open your hands to create a platform or stage for your soul's expression. Visualise a soft, misty ball of light resting on your palms. It has a shape, and you can see inside it clearly. Now ask, 'Please show me my soul's purpose for this lifetime', and wait. Focus on your breathing. Witness the scene that is shown to you, in the light sphere on your hands using your senses to fully engage in every detail. Accept without filtering, reconstructing, or questioning what you are shown, told, or receive through this form of communication.

When you are ready, ask, 'What is my next step toward fulfilling this purpose?' Again, wait to be shown the answer, while maintaining slow, rhythmic breathing. Accept whatever response comes first.

Finally, the last question for this session is: 'What is my soul contracted to learn in this lifetime?' This is a big question; you may only be given part of the answer in this session. Remain connected to the source of your information until the messages have ceased. You can always repeat this exercise later. Thank the source of your communication and ask it to retreat for now.

When you are ready, begin to let the beam of light withdraw from the Third Eye Chakra. Place your hands in your lap. Continue to detach yourself from the universal light source, knowing that you can return to it at any time it suits you. Taking a single deep breath and releasing your connection with the visions you have been holding, begin to return to the present time, in the setting where you began this journey, and make sure you are fully reoriented and aware of yourself and your surroundings before you leave your chair.

The next step is to record the messages you received in a journal, and use them for guidance, contemplation, and reflection. Your soul's purpose may be somewhat surprising to you, and it may take a few days to assimilate and make sense out of the information. Once it has been integrated into your waking knowledge, start to explore how your life mirrors – or fails to mirror – what you have been shown. Explore what steps you can consciously take to start to move toward your purpose. You should support the process by affirming, 'I am willing to honour my soul's contract'. You can further 'power up' the means by which this will happen by affirming, 'I attract all positive opportunities for soul and personal growth'.

Keeping a journal is a useful way of staying focused and highlighting the incidences or events in your life that support your journey.

When you start to make progress, you will notice more readily how the universe supports you. You will draw what you need to yourself, and easily remove old fears or blockages that may have previously formed in your thinking, and therefore become your basis for not acting. Move forward steadily, without rushing, secure in the knowledge that you are being guided and that nothing is left to chance.

In this age of spiritual awakening and soul honouring, our inherent impatience is often our greatest enemy. We are programmed to expect almost immediate tangible results from our efforts. When these do not materialise as expected, we start to question our allegiance to making these worthy changes. Others around us, who are perhaps not engaged in this process of self-discovery and self-improvement, are quick to deflate our ambitions, and even at times criticise or condemn our intentions. This is often a sign that we are on the right path because we are attracting the attention of those who have yet to understand or embrace the fullness of the potential of the human.

*I*n some not-so-rare cases, a soul may fulfill its purpose and choose to leave its host voluntarily although the host still survives. In its place, a 'new' soul takes over and continues the life of the host. For the original host, this opportunity for the incoming soul to 'walk in' to their existence often arrives at a time of great emotional or physical trauma.

We hear of people having 'out-of-body experiences' while undergoing a medical emergency. This is an opportunity for the soul to withdraw and make its way back to its source of origin, and make way for its successor. In some cases the original soul may return to its host and co-exist with the other soul. This can be a harmonious arrangement or in other cases, it may lead to personality disorders and difficulties. Remembering that each soul, when embodied, has a role associated with those of its earthly family and the others whom it meets, it may take some time before the reasons for some traumas and experiences are fully understood. It may take even longer for the family of the 'walk in' to fully understand the new 'character' occupying the familiar exterior.

My experiences with this phenomenon through various clients have enriched my understanding of the mission of a soul. As you would expect, the incoming soul has its own unique purpose, and to the outside world, this may not be an easy transition to accept.

JOSHUA'S NEW LIFE

*M*ost of my clients come to me by way of recommendation, and Joshua was no exception. I met Joshua as a result of his son, Carl. Joshua, a well-built man in his early 60s, presented himself with a firm, 'squash-my-hand-if-you-can' handshake that was accompanied by a broad, warm smile. 'I have been looking forward to meeting you', he said, his tone and volume resonating from his deep baritone voice. 'I understand that you speak straight from the heart, and this is what I need right now'.

'And from the soul', I softly added as I showed him to the consulting room.

Many of us face life-altering traumas and tragedies. When I met Joshua, I had the opportunity to unravel an experience that is common, though not often sought as an explanation for what is being experienced.

'Carl has told me that you have recently suffered a serious heart attack', I began. 'How are you doing now?

'Physically, I am fine, thanks', Joshua replied. 'What he didn't tell you, because he doesn't know, is that after collapsing, I died twice on the way to the hospital. I am very lucky to be here, and I appreciate this fully. I can vividly remember seeing the paramedics working on my body and trying to get my heart started each time it needed help. They were working diligently without panicking. I felt myself hovering weightlessly above, and I was in a place that was very still and silent, but which felt incredibly loving. I heard voices but couldn't make out what was being said'.

'Then, all of a sudden, there was a sharp pain in my chest and a big flash of light – and I don't remember any more than that. Then I woke up in the hospital bed, and I have been trying to make sense of everything since then. I have felt noticeably different. Although I am in the early stages of recovery, it has been three months now, I am no longer driven like I used to be. I am not afraid to get out and enjoy life, yet there is something fundamentally different that I cannot find the words to express and don't fully understand myself. This is why I wanted to talk to you'.

'Tell me about your life before your heart attack', I encouraged. 'Take me though your feelings and thoughts, and your lifestyle'.

'I have worked my entire life chasing one contract after another, until my construction firm was worth millions', he began. 'I gave my wife and son anything they wanted, except my time. I regret that so much. Amanda was such a loving and supportive wife, and she raised Carl almost single-handed.

'Prior to meeting Carl's mother, I was married, but let's just say it didn't work out. When I met Amanda, I was determined to make up for that, and I thought that if I gave them financial security, a fantastic home, holidays, cars, and all the trimmings that everything would be perfect. I worked so hard and achieved a lot. I was called a workaholic, but to me that was a legitimate addiction because I was working for my family. Now I have more than enough money to share, but if it weren't for Carl, I would have nobody'.

Sitting silently, I welcomed Joshua's trust in me. Through his willingness to find the answers, he started to reveal the experiences he had been having recently.

'I can see why I had the heart attack', he admitted. 'Too much work, late nights, bad diet, and occasionally too much booze. I just have so many questions now, and I don't want to make the same mistakes again. How does my story sound to you so far?'

Joshua paused, and so came the first insight.

'The heart is the home of your soul'. I could feel Krisayah's insights coming forth as I told him this. 'Because your soul is a divine spark, it is from here that you can radiate joy and love. This includes love of others, but also love of yourself. If the joy goes out of your life, your heart starts to struggle to function properly. If you practice self-love through maintaining a balance in your life and sharing your time with the people who matter to you, and by nurturing yourself with a health-oriented lifestyle, you do not let the joy go out of your life! So many people work hard for endless years, always thinking of the day they will retire. Their heart is not in their work. There is no joy to fuel this magnificent organ of life, and yet, because of this, it requires more effort, more heart energy, to make sure they keep getting the job done to secure their pension.

The heart cannot run on empty for very long

'The heart cannot run on empty for very long', Krisayah continued, 'and once on the hamster wheel of life, one can only run faster, which ultimately takes its toll. The secret is to place equal effort in the things you enjoy and those you don't, and then to derive equal pleasure and satisfaction from both. A task is always twice as long if your heart is not in it! Be in the moment with everything you do, and you will experience this life-giving magic all around you'.

'Be in the moment!' Joshua exclaimed. 'That would have been a new concept for me six months ago. You might expect someone to be a bit different after what I have been through, however it goes a lot deeper than that. I can understand what you are saying about missing the joy in my life. For years, I didn't question the toll it was taking on me or on my family. But now, I am starting to realize, and I feel I am being guided to do things differently in the future'.

'Since my heart attack, I can remember everything about my life, but now I feel like I am thinking someone else's thoughts. Friends and colleagues who have visited me have all noticed the difference, and they say that my views and sense of humour have changed – for the better I might add! I feel like I have someone older and wiser in me, and when I found myself predicting what a shopkeeper was about to say the other day, I was totally dumbfounded.

'I have always been very down to earth and practical, but now I am drawn to nature, reading, and music, and for the first time, I want to travel and visit my brother in Portugal, and maybe build a home for myself there that could be Carl's one day. I feel like I have been given a new life, and that I have to learn what it is all about one step at a time. This is why I wanted to come and stay with Carl at his lakeside cottage. Not only will it give us chance to spend some time together, but I also feel that I need to be in this environment. I need to be in nature, not surrounded by cement and traffic fumes'.

'It is no wonder that you want to be in this beautiful natural setting,' I explained, 'because our soul rests in the heart and nature asks nothing of us but to be admired and enjoyed. When we connect with nature, and feel the joy swell within us, we awaken the remembering and connection to source'.

'Carl and I don't really know each other that well', Joseph continued, 'so he may not spot the huge differences in myself that I am being told by others are obvious. What I do want is for him to know that I love him very much, and I hope that he forgives me for not being there when he was younger'.

Joshua clenched his thick, calloused, bear-paw hands together tightly as he concluded sharing his thoughts.

'When you say you feel like you have been given a "new life", you might be quite accurate', I said. 'Naturally, when someone experiences a life-threatening event, they take stock and some amend their ways. For you, though, I believe there is a different explanation'.

My mind flickered. The words I was to relay were ready to come forth, but their impact needed to be handled carefully. I paused, centred myself, and focused on opening myself to the source of wisdom that was working through me.

'There is an ancient spiritual phenomenon that corresponds to the experiences you have described', I continued. 'It is more common than one might imagine, and it can have profound effects on the individual. However, it more frequently happens to women. To understand it, we need to first remember that each person has a soul that has its own agenda for each lifetime. On occasion, either through severe emotional or physical trauma, that soul may make use of the opportunity to leave its current host, which it chose for this lifetime. In its place, a new soul enters and carries on the existence of that person.

'The incoming soul may be aware of all the details of the host's life before it took over. This occurrence is called a 'Walk-in'. The fact that you have displayed such distinct changes of character and preference is a strong indicator that this is what has happened in your case. There are known occasions when the original soul doesn't leave, or returns after a few weeks or months, and then both souls co-operate and live within one body'.

Joshua contemplated these words, and then said, 'The old me would have thought you were crazy, and I would have been walking away by now. However, that is the furthest thing from my mind, and I feel totally comfortable with this concept. What other signs are there that would confirm this further?'

'You have listed the main ones', I told him. 'Some people feel compelled to change their lives completely to reflect the character, knowledge, desires, and ambitions of the new soul. They might move to a new area, take on a totally different career, discover exceptional talents they did not have before, or begin to prefer foods that were never palatable previously. They may take up hobbies or interests in response to new found creative or artistic talents. Many experience increased interest and ability in psychic awareness and spiritual development. Some people even go as far as to change their name!'

'Now that's bizarre!' Joshua exclaimed. 'In the last couple of weeks, a work colleague was calling my name and I didn't respond. I heard him, but I didn't think he was addressing me! I felt so stupid when he finally got my attention. I keep hesitating when I am signing my full name, and yet I am not sure what name I should be writing.... It is like I don't know my name anymore!'

'Try not to worry about this', I counseled. 'Your energy, mind, and body are all adjusting to the new identity you are now hosting. It may take a little time for all the pieces of the puzzle to fit together. Be patient. Be aware of your dreams at night, because much information will come to you through them, as this is the best way for your soul to talk to you at the moment. When things have settled down, you may find that your 'gut' instinct is stronger, just as your psychic ability increases. Trust it and go with it; it is all there to help you adjust and do things differently, as you say you want to'.

'Thank you', he said in his deep resonating voice. 'I suddenly feel like I have the keys to a great treasure chest that I know holds many wonderful experiences for me. I feel more connected to the new feelings I have been having, and if what you say is correct, then I will not be afraid to explore my new life, as this all must have happened for a reason. I feel like I truly have been given a second chance now!'

His interest to learn more was obvious, and it seemed that his time with his son would bring healing on many levels. As I opened my diary, I came across a folded flier – tucked inside the front cover – that advertised a 'Spiritual Awakening' seminar the following month in a small city about forty miles away.

I smiled to myself as I thought, 'I cleaned this diary out this morning and this wasn't in there!' I had posted all of the half dozen fliers I had picked up at the health food store near my clinic recently, and given what I thought was the remaining one to Sara when she came for her last appointment. I understood that this was most likely one of those instances when the universe works it's magic, and I didn't see the need to mention this to Joshua as I handed it to him, suggesting that it might be of interest.

Discovering your soul's purpose does not mean that you need to experience extreme situations or forsake everything and everyone you currently hold dear. What it does mean is that through this increased connection to your authentic self, you may find the rough edges of your life starting to smooth themselves. Some people, whose presence in your life has run its course, may drift away; your preferences for food, entertainment, and your lifestyle choices may shift to more genuinely reflect the soul you host.

Once you have this awareness, you have a choice to follow some or all of it, or none of it. That is free will. However, as you might expect, just like any of us, walk-in or not, your joy flows when you follow your soul. Any changes you decide to make are opportunities for growth, and you will be supported throughout this transformational phase by remembering that the universe always acts for your highest good, and that it always supports you. Keep a balance between human sensibility and soul questing as you carefully consider each necessary step along the way. This indicates that you will not forsake anything essential too rashly, or to the total detriment of your health,

Remember that underneath your outward experiences and your conscious rationalizations, your soul is guiding you through your intuition – that gentle, sometimes nagging voice that acts as a guide when you follow your soul's true course. Develop the practice of listening to this wise messenger; acknowledge the feelings in your 'gut' that tell you which direction to follow, and you will find your path richer and more abundant for it.

CHAPTER 10

How to Hear the Voice of Your Soul

CHAPTER 10

How to Hear the Voice of Your Soul

Listen to the stillness of the morning mists;
they speak of the promise of the day.

*W*ith many lifetimes worth of wisdom, knowledge, and insight all available within you, can you imagine how enriched your life would be if you knew how to connect with this amazing wealth?

Achieving this inner communication is easier than you might think. As with most things, it is a matter of knowing the basics and then practicing them at every opportunity, which leverages the connection.

Clear, open communication with your soul's wisdom is the source of true happiness and freedom. So many people maintain the view that life is a battle, a challenge, and a constant fight for survival. In truth, what they struggle against is themselves.

We often hear of colleagues or friends discussing their run of 'bad luck'. Knowing that every thought carries an energy value and weight, when our mindset is heavy with negative ideas and constant dwelling on unfortunate events, we get very stuck very quickly, and this, then, attracts even more of the same like a huge magnet.

Luck, as we call it, can be viewed as an opportunity to experience life's unlimited collection of knowledge. When we listen to the voice of our soul, we will always act in our highest good, which rewards us by what others call luck! When we follow our soul's guidance, we are naturally going to tread our own path, and along the way attract the experiences, confirmations, and rewards of our dedication. This is what makes us authentic, and our journey such an individually enriching experience. When we are inwardly connected, we always act in our own truest interests, or highest good. Without being hard or uncaring, we do not harm our progress by allowing ourselves to be dragged off course by the needs and enticements of others. This is how we then attract our own 'luck', and life follows its course. We face our challenges from a position of deep strength, knowing that any periods of discord are there to bring the next lesson needed for our growth. This is how you would recognise that you are genuinely connected with the gifts of your soul. In reality, this is the closest you will ever come to connecting with your soul, as it is through the expression and voice of its wisdom that it speaks, rather than having a tangible presence with a personality or pulse. Your soul is hitching a ride with you, and through you, and it will share its knowledge with you, in exchange for the experiences it needs to have.

SOUL WHISPERING

Know that we have a connection, and that this will always be true. I am here to guide your life, and in return, to learn from you.

*W*hen you adopt the practice of living by your soul's guidance, you will notice how the struggles of life seem to melt away. In reality, they are still there. However, it is your understanding of them and your perception of their meaning that allows them to carry less detrimental energy and influence. You will fathom the meanings behind events more quickly, and therefore, you will be able to move on from that particular piece of learning, having grown in some positive dimension that will benefit or prepare you for the next phase in your life.

As your relationships become more defined and harmonious, some may alter, others may end, and in their place, you will attract new associations that more truly reflect the energy you give out. Your natural disposition will be one of radiating 'sunshine', and you will be surrounded by a feeling of contentment and bliss that others will comment on regularly.

Without soul connection, life would be meaningless.

This is not to say that you will walk around with a daft grin on your face in a bubble of naivety. Your new-found luminescence is your most attractive attribute, and is also your most protective. You will send out a clear energy signature that only attracts those with a similar one. It is like they have their antenna tuned to the same frequency as the one you are sending. Equally, you will not appeal to others who are on a different wavelength, who cannot receive or understand what you are radiating.

Your soul's message: Without soul connection, life would be meaningless. Without soul communication, life is unsupported. Draw upon this union and be richer for it.

With all this guidance available, it is without doubt that your positive character traits will strengthen and the ones that are perhaps a bit underdeveloped, but would nevertheless serve you well, will also benefit. Negative traits such as jealousy, being judgmental, pettiness, being untruthful at times, and whatever other less-honourable influences that find their way into your thinking and behaviour, or which you attract from others, will soften in time, and be dissolved completely once you realise that your world is far more abundant without these things.

As you connect more frequently with your soul's wisdom and learn to recognise its language, you will never feel isolated or over-challenged by a situation again.

So many people 'beach comb' their way through life. They have their heads down, looking for the odd little thing that interests them, which they then covet until the next thing comes along. After a number of years, they have lots of disjointed experiences, memories, and fragments of their life that naturally do not harmonise. Listening to your soul means that you walk through life with your head up, appreciating the view all around you, taking note of the detail nearby, and yet keeping an eye on the distance. Each day builds on the last; because you are following a carefully guided path, you are free to explore various diversions along the way, knowing that you will ultimately be brought back on track. This is how your soul fulfils its contract, and how you live the life you were meant to.

For the soul to fully experience that which it contracted to in any lifetime, not just yours, it needs to progress through the chosen experiences, emotional states, environmental settings, and whatever else it may have felt necessary in order to help it move nearer to fully understanding the human condition. Our lack of connection with the soul's guidance, combined with our self-satisfying, raw free will, unfortunately helps to ensure that this will happen. When we start to awaken to our own potential as gifted by the soul, we employ a different, more spiritually mature form of free will.

To begin this exploration, we initially need to understand three key facts. First, your soul has been patiently waiting, in fact yearning, for you to start communicating with it. When you know how to 'hear' the voice of your soul and the language it uses, you will realise that it only ever it speaks the truth, with compassion for your highest good. Second, your soul asks nothing of you except 100 per cent trust and patience. These are often the most difficult aspects for us humans to commit to; however, with practice and persistence, it is possible for even the most impatient person to mellow and let the process of trusting show its rewards. Then you will realise that it is the most awesomely powerful act you will ever engage in. Finally, know that there are no wrong decisions when you are following the guidance of your soul. When we genuinely engage in listening to our soul and acting on its wisdom and guidance, we will never be mislead. This can be a hard concept to accept. However, by continually employing the trust that is required, the rewards will quickly follow and reassure us.

SOUL WHISPERING

There are opportunities everywhere. Be open and willing to experience new challenges, and your world will be a very magical and rich place.

*W*hen we are closed off from our soul's voice, we react rather than respond. Every challenge or major decision seems to come from a place of lack and distortion. Knowing that you are supported in every moment by the strength of your soul is like having a personal bodyguard who selflessly looks out for your best interests continually. Detach from this source, and the world becomes a very big, empty place. Feelings of loneliness, detachment, isolation, depression, rejection, and not being understood all characterise a person who is trying to tackle life without this infinite support. Re-connect with your inner source, and life becomes lighter and the path ahead clearer. Each day brings new reasons to trust in the soul's endless willingness to serve.

We know why the soul wants to communicate with us. Now the question to ask at this point is, 'What is the soul trying to communicate?' Searching through the colossal range of possibilities, for me, it comes down to this – the soul reflects itself in the life or world it creates around it. Therefore to help both it and us grow as much as possible, it aims to show us how far we have progressed, and how much further there is to go before we reach enlightenment.

Connecting with your soul's voice is possible through several means. We have already explored how the emotions, which are the expressions of the soul, can influence health, and how the harmony or disharmony of the chakras reveals the condition of the soul energy. In addition, on a easy to observe level, we scan through our wardrobe and take note of the colours of our favourite garments, the styles we chose for different roles we play, and the items that we have had for years that we simply can't discard.

We choose our clothing as a statement, or an expression of our thinking or needs at any given time. We attach emotions and memories to special or favourite pieces, and keep them long after their style is out of fashion or their size no longer fits! All of this is an attempt to hold on to the memories, feelings, or even the people around at that time. We invest something of ourselves in our clothes, and our energy follows naturally.

201

In the late 1980s and '90s, at a time when the economy was booming and 'yuppies' were ticking their way through their 'must-have' lists, women's power dressing was all the rage. Heavily padded shoulders in ladies' suit jackets were intended to portray status and position in their emerging roles in the corporate world, and to a lesser degree, in casual clothes. Women were getting noticed; however, they had to fit in with their male colleagues, and donning a 'status-making' suit helped compensate for the feelings of insecurity that they may have been experiencing.

In reality, for the soul, less is more. When we externally compensate for what we feel we lack internally, we load ourselves with 'all the trappings', which literally act as a trap that holds us in an undeveloped state until we can break free.

For women, when we look at the style of clothes one wears most often, I find that the ones with strong, crisp styling in solid colours, such as one finds in business clothes, are somewhat like armour. These are carefully chosen to provide protection in the most vulnerable places, such as the heart and the solar plexus. This signifies the need to show strength, confidence, ability, influence, authority, reliability, and status where perhaps the wearer feels they need a bit of identity enhancement. There is nothing wrong with this in order to get the ball rolling; however, if the reliance on this kind of 'uniform' is habitual, the person may unknowingly be using their dress code as a block that prevents them from developing the attributes and attitudes that would bring them confidence, self-esteem, respect, and position. While the information above is situational to the workplace, the confirmation of the motive behind clothing choices comes when considering leisure wear. The truest indication of the distance between the role or career identity of a person and their true self is the range of clothes used in each part of their life.

For men, with little flexibility in the corporate dress code, accessories such as jazzy ties, braces, and colourful socks speak the messages from the soul. The language is the same for both sexes. Often seen as 'just a bit of fun', they are confidence boosters, identifiers, and statements of individuality gently calling out for recognition.

For ladies, garments with softer lines, gentle patterns, and mellow colours can equally denote a person who is strong, yet who wants to appear soft, and perhaps even a bit vulnerable. They do not need to wear armour; their inner confidence and self-esteem are well developed and will carry them through. There is an extreme here also, though, and that comes in the form of someone who dresses to portray their vulnerability, their need for dominance, or their weaknesses. They are held in these states by their own life choices, and reflect this in their style through the non-descript colours they choose. It is almost like they want to be invisible by not wearing anything too colourful or noticeable.

This is ultimately a powerful force that subtly pervades our society.

Looking more closely at the colours of the clothes, accessories, and in fact home furnishings you prefer will give you insights as to why you favour certain ones, and also how to put this influence from the soul to its best use as intended.

Fashion trends tend to steer us toward certain colours for the seasons, and also to align with the designers' inclinations. Remember that the people who design, create, and produce your purchases are also working from their intuition and gut instinct, which is their soul's guidance. This is ultimately a powerful force that subtly pervades our society.

As women, when we are shopping, we are attracted by the colour and style of an item, and we know which clothes suit us and which don't. Distinct choices in the colours you choose to wear or have in your home can step outside the standard, trendy designer collections to express something about your individuality and, ultimately, your soul connectedness. Of course, the wearing of any colour for its energy and soul connection can be achieved through your undergarments or jewellery!

The colour red, known to represent prosperity in the East, is worn in the West to state dominance, daring, and at times an aggressive edge. Its wearers use this colour to stabilise themselves and strengthen their foundations. Many men wear rich red socks beneath a smart business suit, which may be a subconscious attempt to feel secure and confident.

More commonly seen on the High Street these days are deep shades of orange that range even to very bright sunburst shades of this most active and creative colour. Wearing these hues denotes a burst of creative energy just waiting to be expressed. Choosing to feature this colour in your daily attire shows that you are listening to one of the major forces of the soul – the need to create. When you next wish to begin a new project or hobby, either wear or surround yourself with a rich orange colour. After a few minutes of quiet contemplation, your creative juices will seem more active, and the project in mind will become a reality with ease. This is because your soul has expanded to bring to you its wealth of talent, and you have aligned with it in this moment.

Venturing further into the shades of true yellow, most people find this a difficult colour to wear comfortably. It is perhaps not surprising that this is the shade associated with claiming your personal power. Equally, this quality is something that most people do not feel comfortable with, based on their upbringing or life experiences. If you are drawn to wear this colour or to accessorise with it, know that your soul is nudging you to gather more confidence in yourself regarding your goals and ambitions. Start to make a life blueprint (see Chapter 11) so that you can fully enjoy the range of your potential. Be mindful of surprise opportunities that come your way, and things that seem like coincidences that are, in fact, soul whisperings urging you to act on the new information you are receiving so that you can take a new direction.

From here, we start to explore the colours that represent more spiritual qualities of our soul's directives. Over the last two or three years, I have been very aware of the trend to combine green and pink. This often takes the form of khaki combat trousers and a pink T-shirt, worn by the best-dressed mannequins in shop windows everywhere, it seems! This combination, speaks of the soul's expression of unconditional love, compassion, and gentle nature, which seeks to practice forgiveness. They represent the attributes of self-worth, self-love, and appreciation, as well as connectedness with the source of true joy – the soul. Neither of these colours is challenging. Like their previously mentioned predecessors, they are inviting, harmonious, and are among the most commonly found combinations in nature. When presenting flowers to an ill friend, these colours make the most healing mixture, which sends vibrations of love and caring based on the frequencies at which these colours resonate.

Moving further into the expressive tones, we arrive at the spectrum of the blue shades. Traditionally worn as business suits to build rapport, confidence within meetings, and to open communication channels, this colour is all about how your soul connects with and receives the outside world. Blue is a 'trust me' colour. It can be either calming or cooling, depending on the tone.

The soul has a basic need to communicate. It does this through several different means, which we are exploring. However, for the host of the soul, it also has a strong need to be heard and to listen, both inwardly and externally, to the guidance it is given. Wearing navy and other blue tones signifies that you are approachable and willing to listen to others. It also beckons for the wearer to be given the attention needed for others to receive their message. However, because communication takes on many forms, this may not be in the verbal sense. It may mean being understood at a soul level, or perhaps appreciated for one's qualities through a random act of kindness or consideration. All of this forms the basis of affirmative communication. Your soul has a voice, and it speaks through you in many ways. Use the shades of blue when you need confidence in approaching a difficult presentation, or when you have something to discuss with a loved one that may not be what they want to hear. You will feel the strength of your soul supporting you, and it will guide you to speak (and act) in your highest good.

As I prepare to teach personal-growth and soul-connectedness seminars, even though there may be dozens of other people around, I can always spot the course attendees as they enter the venue by what they are wearing! Generally, they are attired in variety of violet and lavender shades, sometimes including delicate pink. I always smile when I see these new faces approaching me. I know that, although they may prefer these colours for reasons erring on the side of neutral acceptance, they are already connected with their soul, and the smile on their face confirms this to be true.

The purple shades, from the deepest indigo to the softer lavenders, speak of inner connectedness. This is the colour of intuition, the internal language of the soul. To wear these hues shows that you are centred, self-accepting, and content with your life, although it may present challenges. It indicates that you are willing to surrender (for the most part) to the guidance from within. Clothing worn in business does not often feature the colour purple, although it is more apparent in logos and advertising these days. I sense that this is because many companies portray their mission statements to be all encompassing of the work/life balance, and as such, their company colours aim to reflect this more wholesome, less money-driven agenda. In China, purple and gold or yellow are known as the Emperor's colours, which represent personal power, wealth, and inner wisdom in perfect harmony. These two colours can work well in home furnishings and art, though as a fashion statement, there could be some explaining for the wearer to do!

Moving on to the ultimate representation of all colours combined, we have the radiance of white. This is the attractor of all positive energy. Spiritual teachers, gurus, religious leaders, and brides all don this purest of colours, which in reality is the combination of all the colours already mentioned. This is the seat of our connectedness to the source. Our soul has continual, direct communication with the Creator, and the highway on which this exchange happens is a luminous white beam of light. Wearing all white can seem to say 'look at me' a bit blatantly in some cases. However, it is also the sign of someone who is truly connected with their soul and who is enriched by the strength of this relationship. So why not 'look at them'? Their radiance may just spark something in the onlooker that echoes deep within and awakens the voice of many lifetimes.

By far the most spiritually significant colour at this time is turquoise. That rich blend of blue-green hues that unites the sky with the waters of our world and echos a balance and connection between earth and the universe. Evident now as a newly visible colour in the rainbow spectrum, that the more spiritually aware of are able to see these days, this is the vibration that takes your own resonance higher. If you are drawn to have this colour around you, then you are being signalled to from your soul that you are ready for awakening. You are probably already aware of this in some way, have faith in your inner feelings and follow your instincts, you will not be misled.

Worth mentioning, too, are brown and black, neither of which is found in the rainbow spectrum of the soul because they do not carry or reflect light. Brown shades speak of a connection with the earth, of being grounded and anchored. This is fine, however, if the dominant colour in your life is beige or brown, then perhaps you need literally to 'lighten up'. These colours are unchallenging and allow the wearer to melt into the background and avoid being too readily noticed. By choosing brighter colours, or at least accessorising with them, you will raise your level of vibration, and your energy levels will follow.

Black is the lack of all colour, and it absorbs light without reflecting any at all. It draws negativity easily to it. Although very stylish and almost an essential in any wardrobe, it carries a strong energy signature that is not in tune with the soul or spiritual expansion and expression. Save it for those occasions that require it, and accessorise with bright colours to add some sparkle to increase the light energy you carry.

So, your wardrobe is not just filled with nice designs, functional garments, and comfortable gear to suit your lifestyle and mood. It is a chorus of guidance and reflection from your soul. Look at the items that you hang onto when fashion and your dress size have long since passed them by. When you hold this item separate from the rest, notice what feelings it evokes within you. This is reminiscent of your soul talking to you from the time when you chose it or last wore it.

We may feel that if we give these items away, and cast this and other similar precious things into a new life via the numerous charity shops that benefit from our clutter-clearing, that we are somehow loosing part of our past and ourselves. In reality, when we strengthen our clear and regular contact with our soul, we can connect with these feelings at will. This means that the energy that is bound up in the material goods will be returned to us, enabling our life to be so much more vibrant and self-empowered.

If you really want to know what your soul is trying to say to you, go through your wardrobe! Sort out the mundane in favour of the emotionally charged garments. Then spend time with each of the items. Perhaps journal what feelings your favourite pieces stir within you, and then sit back and reflect on the messages that your soul is trying to convey. Do you have clothes that you wear when you want to feel confident? Is there an outfit that guarantees a great day every time you wear it?

I once walked along a section of the Great Wall of China wearing my 'Timmy Tiger' t-shirt! The child-like drawing of a funny-looking tiger that fills the surface of this, my favourite garment, always makes me smile, and I know that I am going to have a great day when I wear it! Every day should be a 'Timmy Tiger' t-shirt day!

Don't worry if the colours that generate strong feelings within you don't match the guidelines above, because they are only given as a starting point. What is important is that you register the messages from your soul and then do something about them.

Check with yourself to see if you have taken note of these inner whisperings. If you have, then the item may not hold such significance to you. However, the fact that you still get a stirring of memories or emotions when you hold it in front of you or try it on shows that you have not yet quite captured its message or integrated it into your life. Clothes that simply make you feel good are there to tell you that you have this capability within you all the time. You do not need to put on a certain item to bring this to the surface; it is just a physical reminder of how you can connect with your joy continually. You already hold all of this within you.

Refer to your journal and the guidance above, and ask yourself how you could nurture the necessary wisdom from within. When you are able to let go of items from years ago, you free yourself to live in the now! This is very empowering.

I remember when my Gran died. She had a particular calf-length, heavy tweed skirt that I thought was particularly lovely. The colours were rich; the weave was kind of chunky, making it the type of shirt she would have worn on Sunday afternoon walks in sensible shoes. I never intended to wear it. I just liked having it because it made me feel close to her. I kept that skirt for years. It travelled across from Canada to the UK with me, and was lovingly – almost ceremonially – placed at the top of my suitcase that held my seasonal change of wardrobe.

On one occasion, when it was time to pack away the winter clothes, I tried on this skirt. This confirmed that I was hanging on to it in an attempt to hold onto a piece of her and what she liked. I savoured the memories of my lively, 'game for a laugh', but gentle, Grandmother as she would have been. In that moment, I had confirmation that part of her character was alive in me, and that it was time for this item to be birthed into new life and be bundled off the charity shop. This was not an act of disregard for her or the quality of the garment, just a nudging from my soul telling me that, in order to move forward, I would have to let go. Now, perhaps, when others are tamed by their sensibilities, I am the one willing to try new things. As I get older, I find this keeps me young, just like my Gran must have felt!

The essence of the feelings attached to a particular item – whether it is clothing, home furnishings, bricks and mortar, a mechanical device, or covered in jewels – can always be retained within. Allowing this to happen it adds to your radiance because you are enriching your soul, which always shines brighter than any star.

In listening to your soul as described, you are, in fact, listening to your intuition. This strong inner voice, which is so often ignored, is seen as a quality of the great mystics. Each and every one of us, however, was born with a finely tuned, clearly resonating inner voice. It is our conditioning and early experiences that silence this most truthful and caring guide.

Our intuition is exactly that – in(ner)tuition. It exists to guide and teach us, through the choices it helps us make, toward the life we were meant to live. All too often, our decisions are mere responses to some fear-driven motive. We think we might miss out if we do or do not respond to a situation or circumstance in a particular way. Often, when faced with these times, if we take a step back, we will see that, first of all, whoever wants us to make a certain decision is the person who will primarily benefit. Yes, you too may get something you want out the commitment you are about to make, but it may not be weighted in your favour.

At a time when you are struggling to decide what course of action to take, the biggest favour you can do for yourself is to take a step back and find some time to sit quietly. Then, without analysing the actual situation, ask inwardly, 'Am I acting in my highest good if I decide to...?' You will get an answer, probably in your own voice. Take it. Do not try to second guess it or argue with it if you do not like the reply. Yes, it is true that there are no wrong decisions. This is because no matter what choices you make, your soul will always aim to keep you on course. However, why knowingly make life more difficult or put yourself in the way of unwanted stress, financial hardship, relationship strain, or whatever learning curves not listening to your intuition will bring?

When presented with convincing facts, our logical left brain tries to override our softer-spoken right brain. It is the intuition – housed in the Third Eye Chakra, which is located in the space between the eyebrows – that acts as a mediator because it sits nicely between both hemispheres of the brain. It knows what is in your best interest, as it listens to the creative, nurturing qualities of your right side and foresees what the intellect of the left cannot.

Learning to listen to your intuition takes a bit of practice. It is best to start with relatively small decisions. What to wear, for instance, or what to eat, and then, when you have gained some confidence, how to respond to a choice or decision. It all comes from asking a simple question: 'Which is my best choice in this circumstance that will be in alignment with my highest good?' You will receive the answer through your feelings, emotions, and energy centres. When you act based upon your intuition, you connect with your most authentic expression of yourself – your soul. It all fits neatly together in a self-supporting, life-enhancing synergy.

The keys to connecting with your intuition are easy to follow when practiced in this order:

Be willing to trust your intuition.

Make time each day to sit quietly, even for a minute. Breathe deeply, and allow yourself to feel calm, centred, and more focused.

Connect with nature regularly, and fully appreciate what your senses soak up –this will enhance your inner senses.

Ask your inner guide for its wisdom regularly.

Be watchful for a response. It may come as a word, in your own voice, in your mind; it might come through your feelings or emotions; or, it might present itself through your dreams.

When you receive an insight, do not question or challenge it. Simply trust and accept it, and act upon it.

When the gift of your intuition has been imparted, sit quietly, offering thanks and gratitude. This is the sure and certain way to strengthen the connection.

Above all, use it. You were born to live a rich, supported, and exciting life. Your intuition is your travel agent on this journey.

CHAPTER 11

Living Your Dreams

CHAPTER 11

Living Your Dreams

You already have everything within you to achieve what you desire. You are everything.

We have more resources available to us today than at any other time in the history of the human race, and yet through our beliefs and conditioning, we hold ourselves in suspended animation and deny ourselves the life we were meant to live.

What would your life be like if you truly believed that you could have, be, or do anything you desired? Stop for a moment and think about this. Where do you see yourself? What is happening in the life of your dreams?

Everything begins with a thought. If you are able to create a vision, even for a few moments, of a life you would like to experience, then it is possible! Even though you think that you could never achieve what is in your heart, have enough money or resources to change your life dramatically to match your vision, or have the support from those near and dear to you, if you hold a vision clearly in your mind, then you will start to move toward making it a reality each and every day.

How is this possible? Let me show you.

First of all, what does it really mean to live the life of your dreams? Each of us has a right to explore the opportunity for soul satisfaction. This is why we are here, now, at this time of great planetary evolution, abundance, and awakening. To wake up in the morning and know that it will be a great day filled with enriching experiences that will bring a wealth of joy, companionship, and just enough challenge to spark your creativity – this is a typical day in your 'dream' world.

SOUL WHISPERING

The excitement you feel swelling up from within is coming from your soul, as you unite with the infinite within you.

*L*iving the life of your dreams involves feeling continually fulfilled. This may come about through how you occupy your time, whom you choose to spend it with, how you express yourself, what you are able to contribute, pay forward, or give back, and what legacy you create that marks your time in this life.

You can tell when someone is living how their soul intended just by looking at them. Their posture is strong and upright, they smile effortlessly and bring the best out in others, and they have an energy field around them that oozes self-confidence, though they are not arrogant or showy. Some might comment that these people seem to 'have all the luck'. In reality, what they have is the belief that they can have, be, and do anything that takes their interest. This includes the full range of possibilities expressed through spiritual connectedness, harmonious relationships, and financial and material comfort.

You host a source of incredible potential.

When you walk amongst shoppers, notice how they carry themselves. Although they may be tired and weary, someone who has nailed their next step toward a life of their dreams does not shuffle, with eyes turned down, or wear a frown!

Your soul's message: You host a source of incredible potential. Let yourself connect with this through affirming only positive outcomes to the ideas and ambitions you hold.

Starting to work toward creating the life of your dreams is a tremendously empowering experience. The most important thing to remember is that it is the journey that brings the rewards, not the destination. Equally, depending on how dramatically you feel you need to change some or all aspects of your life, remember that it takes time, and that there will be challenges along the way.

SOUL WHISPERING

At the point when you see the only option as retreat, you are at the crest of an amazing leap forward. Seize it, embrace it, take that risk, and be thankful that your soul held the vision to guide you to this crucial moment.

*C*onditioning is the reason why most people do not realise that they are literally masters of their own destiny. Our parents, grandparents, and every generation that preceded them framed reality within the current thinking and events of the day. Trends and traditions, expectations and obligations, as well as political, cultural, and social unrest all serve to stifle the soul, preventing it from being truly empowered. We have grown up with this legacy; in fact, our DNA carries the energy imprint of these past generations. Although our soul is a visitor across many lifetimes, each host it chooses has its own genetic pre-programming, along with a spirit, that collectively act as navigator, driver, and mechanic for this vehicle we call our life.

Our soul needs to learn its chosen lessons for each lifetime. It can achieve this most effectively when the individual opens him or herself to the widest possible expression of their uniqueness. This is why creating the life of your dreams is essential for your soul's benefit.

Many people run their lives as though it owes them something. They expect certain achievements by specific ages. Using this false measure detracts from the richness of the journey toward wholeness and happiness. When your life seems full of challenges or 'bad luck', the temptation is to cast blame on others, or on the circumstances that we think cause and control our fate. The truth is that the responsibility is our own.

We created our current reality with every decision we have ever made, and we can change it in the same way. All the complaining and disassociating from our circumstances is futile. In fact, what this does is set our radar to detect only situations that match what we are complaining about. Like attracts like. In these cases, when the light is shone on a possible path toward a better reality, fear of change rears its head and shouts, 'Stop! Who do you think you are to be contemplating that?'

Many people, although they are unhappy in their lives, would rather have things stay as they are than set about changing anything. Why does fear have such a strong hold on us? Fear is like a safety valve designed to make us question our ideas and intentions, urging us to 'play safe' and stay where we are. I have always tried to live by the words, 'Do not let fear run your life'.

And yet we are bombarded daily with fear-inducing stories on the news, from our insurance companies, and in the magazines that tell us the latest 'must haves', and how to look if we are to be considered valid human beings. Fear, the mass controller, has no place in a life of your dreams. If fear can have any role, let it be one of motivation toward being more authentically alive in everything you do and say.

When I am working with clients to help them start to create the life they want, there are some common fears that creep into their thinking. Concerns that their close relationships might change or breakdown, that they do not deserve a better lot, that they might not be capable of achieving what they set out to, that they will become too successful or too busy, that they might achieve beyond their parents or siblings expectations, and finally that they might be seen as elitist or self-excluding by following their own path.

In reality, things do change – that's the whole point! Relationships can become stronger, because those close to you will subtly learn by your example. If resistance is met, then this highlights the fears in others. This can bring out controlling behaviour, and yet with considerate communication, and explanations to soften the anxieties around you, you can garner support. Self-generated fears are only calls for more contemplation and achievement-oriented thinking. Many 'what ifs' and unfounded problems are in fact ones brought about by the fear of being successful, not of failing.

Getting started is the most exciting part! You can see your new life, but how do you get there from the reality you know so well right now? The best way to start to create this wonderful life that is waiting for you is to take a pen and notepad and write two columns. Title the first, 'My dream life'. In this column, you are going to describe, in detail, what your 'dream life' is all about. Title the second column, 'Transferable knowledge, skills, talents, resources, and abilities'. Here, you are going to list your character traits, experiences, learning, and any other strengths that can help you make this transition.

Below is the account of where Mandy, a twenty-eight-year-old account executive for a busy advertising firm, began her life changes. Her story is common, and her situation had become so ingrained in her energy that her health was reflecting it, and calling to her to make some changes.

'My problem is that I feel totally stuck in life', Mandy told me. 'I am only twenty-eight. I feel so unfulfilled, like I am wasting my time in everything I do. My job pays well, it's interesting, I get to travel, and I have reasonably good lifestyle, however it is just not me! I hate it and can't seem to find the sparkle inside me anymore. I have wanted to change jobs, but I haven't found anything that appeals to me. This is why I was hoping you could help me'.

Mandy excused herself to try to blow her nose and grumbled that her sinuses had been blocked for weeks now.

'When we hold strong emotions and ideas – consciously or subconsciously – for a long time, one of the avenues through which they manifest is our health', I explained to her. 'This is one way that the soul talks to us. Most of us, however, consider illness and disease as an inconvenience, and something to be released from as quickly possible. When this happens, we often return to the same or greater ill health later because the message of the illness has not been acknowledged and learned from fully.

'By co-relating where a person is experiencing illness, it is possible to reliably interpret where one is holding blocked energy in their thinking, views, or mindset that is restricting them from manifesting their full potential. The mid region of your face, where your sinuses are, represents and reflects 'all that you presently are'. Your feelings of being stuck have translated into a condition that, in itself, represents being congested and stuck. Just like your sinuses, the natural flow in your life has temporarily ceased and this has resulted in you feeling frustrated and unable to move forward. I imagine this condition came into existence a short time before you became aware of the depths of your mindset?

'When I think back', Mandy mused, 'I realise you're right.... It started about a month before I first spoke to anyone about it. And when I got it all off my chest, it was better for a few days, but then it built up again'.

'This is because you released some of the trapped emotional energy, but did not change the mindset or energy that fuelled it', I informed her.

'So how do I do that?' she wondered.

'Listen to your language to start with', I counseled. 'Every time you let your mind become filled with negative thoughts, or when you repetitively speak about being stuck and directionless, you add to the physical sinus congestion, and metaphorically keep yourself where you don't want to be. Take control of these saboteurs. Begin to change your internal dialogue, and be totally aware of what thoughts might be fuelling your situation. For the benefit of you and your soul, you could start to create your own life blueprint. It is a very valuable exercise that can be supported by affirmations.'

'I will guide you in the four steps, and then you will be able to start to take control of your life and create the future you desire.'

'Step one is to create a 'List of Your Dreams, Aspirations and Ambitions'. this is where you commit to writing everything you want in your life. Creating this list of ideas allows you to objectively gather all the random wishes about how you would like your life to be. Don't hold back. However, make sure that what you include on your list is genuinely what you wish to manifest. It should include the type of role you see yourself, what you would like people to remember you for, what you would like to create and own, what lifestyle you want, and even where you would like to travel.'

'Make sure that your 'dream list' contains things that are current, rather than goals that perhaps were relevant years ago, but are still on your mind through habit or familiarity. To do this, find yourself a quiet place and let your pen fill the paper. If you have trouble, start by imagining that the world of possibilities is yours for the asking and that there are no restrictions. Say to yourself, 'Now that I am fully confident and without restriction in any way, this is what I would like to do with my life....'

'You may want to focus on just one aspect of your life first. In your case, direct your thoughts to your career. List what would really bring you satisfaction, and what ambitions and interests you have held that could now become a source of fulfilment and income. Also list any talents, training, or experience you do have that could be used to nurture a new direction. Get everything out on paper. Don't filter anything; just let your ideas flow and see where it leads you. Then list your skills, knowledge, and abilities that can be used to help make your dream a reality.'

'Step two is to select which of your dreams or career interests appeal most to you. You may have more than one that appeals to you, so you need to evaluate each one for its appropriateness in accordance with your soul's purpose and journey by connecting with your sense of inner knowing. To do this, write the shortened list of your dreams or ideas on a piece of paper or in a notebook, leaving space between each one. Then, sit quietly, alone, breathe deeply, read the first item on your list, and hold it in your mind as you close your eyes and think of nothing else.'

'In your mind, ask, "Is this the most correct path for me to follow at this time?" Listen for the answer. It may come immediately. It may be in your own voice, or another's. Whatever the reply, do not question it. Open your eyes momentarily and record the response without analysing it. Read the next item on the list, close your eyes, ask the question (or depending on the answer to the previous question, rephrase it if that is appropriate), and repeat this process until you have answers to every consideration. You can use this method to discover further information about the most desirable path to follow, once you have determined it. You might ask where you should start to look for guidance, information, or training, whom you need to speak with, or whether this is the right town or city in which to build your future dream.'

'Allow your self-esteem to see that anything is possible; you just have to choose which path or dream to manifest. It might be that you have always derived great pleasure and a feeling of wholeness from working with a particular group of people, with animals, in the arts, or with technology. Whatever brings a swell to your heart is worth exploring further.'

'Step three is to put your plan into action. Once you have determined which path to follow, leave these thoughts and your notes alone for a few days. When you come back to them, notice how you feel. If you get a rush of excitement and feel eager to get started working your way toward realising these goals, then you are on the right path for certain. If not, return to the questioning process to ascertain what is the most correct route to follow at this time.'

'The next step requires you to look at the big picture of getting from where you are presently to where you want to be. See yourself as having already achieved your dream, and then write down in detail what that picture contains. You could cut out pictures in magazines to help you depict this vision. Describe the whole setting or scene, including how you are dressed and how you feel. This vision is what you are aiming for; by adding your emotions and sensory input, you add more energy to its reality.'

'Now, look at the distance between your vision and where you are now. Jot down what the differences are in terms of what you may need to learn, change, increase, reduce, gather around you, or explore in order to be able to stand in your vision. Arrange this list in a logical, sequential order. You might recognise the need for some new training or skills. You might also need to rekindle some contacts, or make new ones to help you make these changes.'

'Whatever it takes, generate a comprehensive list that can be used as a set of initial markers of achievement, or mini-goals. Next, so that the whole process does not seem too outfacing, break each of your goals down into a list of daily tasks, like making certain phone calls, speaking to resourceful people, researching contacts, and so forth. Go to your calendar or diary and plan in when you are going to do this groundwork. Plot each component of the list of things you need to do to get to where you want to be.'

'You will quickly see that by achieving each list of daily tasks, you are moving nearer to manifesting your dream, so that at the end of each day, you have moved forward – or at least tried to – and you now know what you have to do tomorrow. Your calendar becomes your timescale planner and motivator. You can start to see it becoming a reality once you have dates in mind by which you aim to achieve the initial few steps that underpin the achievement of one of your dreams. This will fill you with such focus and enthusiasm that nothing will be able to stop you.'

'When we are on the right track, everything will flow. It is only when we are pushing something uphill that we experience resistance, and this is a sign that perhaps we need to redefine our approach to completing this part of our vision manifestation. You might find, after taking the initial few steps, that you realise that this particular dream or aim is not really what you wanted after all. Do not despair; you were guided down this path for a reason.'

Anything is possible if you listen to your heart and chart a steady course

'Take some time to review what you have learned so far, as there will be a nugget of great value within it that you may not have acquired otherwise. This will most likely be a key factor when you latch into your true path. Return to your initial list, and ask your inner guide, your soul, for direction once again. No effort honestly extended is ever wasted'.

'I have been rekindling my interest in my painting and drawing pastime lately', Mandy informed me, 'and I would love to do something with that. Do you really think it could be possible?'

'Anything is possible if you listen to your heart and chart a steady course toward your goal', I answered. 'Your greatest tool is to use affirmations. For example, if you wanted to lose weight, you would say to yourself several times a day, "I am the most ideal weight for my frame and good health". Once you "tune" your thinking to what you desire, your actions and awareness co-operate to make certain that you see all the possibilities that will lead to your goal manifesting. You could include some other, more general affirmations, as these help draw in positive energy to support your intentions. Put these statements into your own words to give them greater potential: "I embrace each day ready for new experiences"; "I allow my creativity to be fully present in everything I do"; and "I am working in the most perfect career, which matches my personality, talents, and ambitions, and exceeds my financial expectations".

Mandy's expression told me that she could imagine the benefits of such an exercise. However, the involuntary shuffle she made at my last comment told me that she was not totally comfortable with this concept. Confirming my thoughts, she sought clarification.

'But I am not working in my most perfect career!' she exclaimed. 'How long will it take?'

'Not yet!' I agreed. 'In order for change to manifest, you need to create the opportunity for it to find you. If you imagine that every thought – good or bad, happy or sad – is a different coloured light beam, when you let them shine, you are going to attract the people, circumstances, and opportunities that recognise and resonate with each particular beam. Thus, what you put out, you attract back'.

If you project that you hate your job, all you are going to attract to yourself is more awareness and reasons why you hate your job because that is what your light beam is showing you. Affirming that you work in the most perfect career does two things. First, it makes the negative energy around your current situation less dense, and second, it signals to the universe that you are ready to cast a different light to attract the career that would most meet your soul's needs and purpose for this lifetime. Does this make sense?' I asked.

Mandy's agreement came in the form of a nod and a smile.

'Once you start', I continued, 'watch for the signs. I generally find that it takes about a month of diligent consciousness toward our goals before changes start to happen. You must be open to the fact that in order to get where you are intended to be, there may be a few rough patches along the way. Hold your vision clearly, and you will know what action to take when it is required. When you start to radiate more positive energy, you will naturally attract the same. In relation to your work, you will notice the opportunities, meet people, and experience signs from the universe that most people call coincidences, which will support your new thinking. Ultimately, you will know when you are on the right track and no longer stuck because your sinuses will reflect this shift.'

Our first session gave Mandy the tools to start to carve out the life she wanted. Within two weeks, when we next met, she had taken some time off work to focus on her 'dream life' planning. She was exuberant when we next met, and although she realised that she needed to stay at her job for a while yet, she had enrolled in an evening art class and was anticipating featuring some of her work in a small, local art show to be held in six months time. Clarity, motivation, and a bit of guidance were all that Mandy needed to break free from the congestion in her life. True confirmation of her successful time spent investing in her future was evident by the lack of sinus problems on her second visit.

Mandy, like all of us, held inside herself the keys to unlock the door to an amazing life. If you are stuck, frustrated, under expressed, or carry a burning ambition, use these steps to release what your soul wants you to know and take up that pen and paper. Making a beginning takes one second, and from there it will flow. If you need to get used to the idea of creating the life of your dreams, start by addressing something smaller than a complete overhaul of your life. Perhaps you want to lose weight, change your car or home, and make your current living environment more nurturing. Approach any of these smaller aspects of your life in the same way, and it will then be easier to face the bigger goals and ambitions you hold.

Remember, failure sometimes is going to happen. However, it is only an altered outcome from the one you imagined! It is really success in a different form. There is learning to be gained from every experience, and this is what makes the journey a ride not to be missed.

CHAPTER 12

Soulistic Empowerment

CHAPTER 12

Soulistic Empowerment

When the moment arrives, spread your wings and take flight.

*H*ow wonderful to be alive at a time when there is more life-improving guidance and potential than any generation before us has been lucky enough to have available. Daily, individuals in every walk of life are waking up to the reality that they create their own destiny, health, wealth, and happiness. We have an abundance of healers, therapists, and coaches poised to guide and untangle our lives and help us weave a path forward into a state of being more whole, complete, and content. Yet, for many, the awareness, willingness, resources, time, obligations, and commitments do not permit even the first steps of a life overhaul to take place.

Soulistic Empowerment is a state of being. It is not measured by one's material wealth, yet for some it might be reflected through it. Instead, this soul-honouring mindset embraces the richest concepts of conducting and directing your life as it was meant to be. By increasing your self-confidence and self-esteem through soul consciousness, your own uniqueness becomes your strength. Soulistic Empowerment allows you to live authentically in your own truth.

SOUL WHISPERING

Sip slowly at the source that nourishes your soul. Although endless, it is worth savouring.

*Y*our soul has an agenda of learning for this lifetime. This may not always mean that everyday will be rosy, and in truth there may be times of great challenge. Equally, there is every opportunity for the majority of your days to be blissful, enchanted, and uplifting.

Whether we experience adversity, sudden bereavement, injustice, failure, violation or privilege, contentment, abundance, or opportunity, there is soul-affirming learning to be gained. When life is harsh, we can easily let our emotions and energy become burdened and heavy, meaning that we can only see the depths of darkness that surround the issue at hand. At times when life is buoyant, joy-filled, and carefree, we often forget that there is learning to be gained here also.

When one is living soulistically, there is a deep connection with one's inner core of centeredness and wisdom. We can see 'the bigger picture'. With the energy of the soul pulsing through our cells, we anchor our reality to our innate understanding that we are here for a reason. This certainty brings freedom to explore and experience life on a different level. It means that although we experience our lives on a human translation basis (by interpreting everything at a personal, emotional, or personality level), we are able to extend our soul consciousness to avoid becoming over grounded and often damaged by singular moments or events.

231

You will recognise this united state not by choruses of angels singing overhead in your praise, or by a huge lottery win that places you on a new millionaires list, but by a deep sense of tranquility emanating from your deepest heart core. You will find beauty in simplicity. Nature will present you with the richest sensory experience imaginable. You will frame the world and the actions of others in the context of observational empathy, and remove all need to judge or criticise. You will accept yourself, in all your realities and forgive the actions, thoughts and deeds that may have been less light-filled in the past, knowing that the 'soulful you' is the true expression of your reason for being.

Your soul's message: The wisdom and knowledge of your soul brings the potential to make this life everything you want it to be.

Through Soulistic Empowerment, one gains life enrichment, and visa versa. This symbiotic, synergistic relationship fuels a natural disposition toward positive self-regard. It lays the cornerstones for increased self-worth, self-esteem, radiant confidence, vibrant health, and ultimately unconditional love of self and others. In generating life enrichment through Soulistic Empowerment, there is no fertile soil for the weeds of guilt, blame, fear, anger, regret, resentment, or bitterness to germinate.

If you want to make changes in your life, but are not sure how to go about it, then working from a perspective of Soulistic Empowerment can open the door and show you the way. If you feel stuck or abandoned by life, learning how to tune into your inner guide will bring clear direction to help you take that next step. When you connect with your soul, your life begins to move in direction most supported by the universe and the divine.

There are three keys to Soulistic Empowerment. The first is to know that our lives are a direct reflection of our thoughts. Second, that there is learning to be gained in any given situation or circumstance. Third, is that to benefit and to honour the first two keys, one has to act on the knowledge and opportunities that arise.

As your soul is working toward being of service to the greater needs of humanity, to awaken your personality to the messages and gifts this eternal energy force brings means that, ultimately, you are contributing to the spiritual evolution of all mankind. It does not mean that by honouring your soul's reason for manifesting in this lifetime that your experience of this life will be cut short. The pay back is that you get to live more of your life in a state nearer total happiness and joy. The longer you ignore the callings of your soul, the greater proportion of your days will be spent struggling and facing repeated battles until the learning is received.

When we are not living soulistically, we adopt coping strategies such as blaming others or external circumstances for our current position in life. We do not take responsibility for what we attract, and therefore we distance ourselves from the power to make the necessary changes that would bring about the very things we desire.

SOUL WHISPERING

When challenges face you, remember that there is learning to be gained. Learn the lesson, and you can move on.

To connect with the gifts of Soulistic Empowerment, we need to be permanently mindful of the keys mentioned previously, and employ their wisdom. First, become aware of your current situation and your thoughts regarding it. If you are experiencing financial difficulty, explore your feelings about your own self-worth. Where did these ideas come from? Were you brought up in a household where you were told that you did or did not deserve what you got? Was money treated as a threat to being a good and respectable person? No doubt there are other issues or beliefs that are hardwired into your thinking that currently define your reality, and thus the thoughts you put out.

Find yourself some quiet time, and make a list of the areas in your life that are not as you would like them to be. This list may include certain beliefs, such as, 'I am not worth loving', or 'As my parents did not display affection, I am incapable of giving and receiving this myself'. These, and many other ingrained thoughts, were made at a time when we had no other experience, perhaps as a young child. However, as an adult, no doubt with the experience of these beliefs reflected in our own relationships, we have a choice to continue thinking this way, or to spiritually wake up and listen to the voice of your soul.

Take this list, and for each comment, write a positive counterstatement that feels comfortable, or at least generates a sense of possibility within your heart. Then each day, read through your second list, again and again, until you start to see subtle changes occurring. It can take a bit of time for this to start – usually about twenty-eight days – but keep going. If nothing else, it is better to occupy your thinking time with positive possibilities rather than negative nonsense.

Second, when you reflect on your previous or current experiences, you may find that there is a pattern that becomes obvious. It is true that the universe will repeatedly send opportunities to learn a particular lesson until you have made the necessary mental and energetic shift to absorb this learning. So, if you find that your relationships end in the same way time and time again, it could be, perhaps, that you attract, as a reflection of your inner self, the same kind of person continually. Inevitably, the partnership will unfold in the familiar manner, which will reinforce the non-serving conviction you hold. Look to yourself, your beliefs, and your needs to recognise the patterns you practice.

SOUL WHISPERING

Deep within us is a spiritual anchor that holds us fast as we test how far the chain of life's opportunities will let us venture from our chosen, original mooring.

*T*aking a look at yourself in this light can be tough, and you may find yourself slipping into feelings of embarrassment, self-blame, failure, and guilt. Stop there. These drops of self-poison serve no purpose on the route to Soulistic Empowerment. Just as positive emotions have energy, so too do negative ones. Reaffirm the ones that make you feel good about yourself and focus on these. It is all too easy to wallow in self-destructive thinking. In fact, because of the 'heaviness' of these thoughts, they almost create a sticky comfort zone that acts like a magnet to your next thought and responses to life. Someone could offer you a golden opportunity, and your immediate response might be one of doom and gloom, just waiting for the rug to be pulled out from underneath your feet. This pit of despondency acts like a vacuum, and unless you start to make conscious changes in your thinking, you will be rewarded with confirmation that you cannot trust life.

Catch yourself when these moments of self-limitation arise. Acknowledge what you are thinking in the first instance by saying to yourself, 'I could respond negatively, however I choose to look at this situation as an opportunity for growth, self-improvement, and soul honouring'. Make this your natural approach, and it won't be long before you drop the need to recognise your habitual negative thinking and just focus on the best and most soul-serving approach to whatever life brings to you.

Why does it take about twenty-eight days for changes to start to become noticeable? This is the duration of the lunar cycle, the ebbing and flowing of the magnetic forces exerted by the moon on the earth and its inhabitants. During this regular succession, the body goes through its stages of creation, regeneration, and dissolution. In this time frame, many of the tissue cells regenerate. We know that science has proven that thoughts and emotions create chemicals that allow cells to communicate and form their behavioural character. As new cells replace the old, they carry the energy of the new thoughts and replace the old ones in a natural progression of internal evolution. Thus, adopting a consistent practice of focusing on positive, life-affirming attitudes and beliefs allows every cell in your body to eventually represent this soul-serving mindset.

SOUL WHISPERING

In these times of accelerated spiritual awakening, there may be days when you think you may never reach a certain level of understanding, or inner connection. Do not measure yourself against others. You are not living their life or travelling their journey. We each have our own unique contributions to make. You are leaving the footprints of your soul in the sands of time. Dance on!

$\mathcal{T}$he first stage of reflection naturally leads to the second stage of awareness, and the final strategy to empower your soulistic life is to acknowledge and act on that which you have learned. Be mindful of a period of confirmation following the adoption of your new mindset and internal structure. Initially, there will inevitably be occasions to strengthen your inner world brought to you lovingly from the outer reality. Once you have solidified your empowered wisdom framework, you will no longer attract the circumstances that bring these challenges. Instead, you will be given opportunities, for the benefit of your soul or others around you, to demonstrate your attributes of Soulistic Empowerment. This will come in the form of increased self-confidence, self-worth, and self-esteem, along with attracting what you most desire and focus on to enrich your life.

Soulistic Empowerment brings life enrichment, which means that you can truly 'Be as your soul'. In doing so, you become a formidable force of soul-directed energy that ignites a world of infinite possibilities within your reality. In this way, you are living a harmonious, balanced life that nurtures your experiences and brings joy and delight effortlessly and endlessly. To be as your soul, you are filled with light, loving, and wisdom. You embrace life with a deep serenity that speaks volumes of your connectedness to the truth and your definition of yourself and your inner truth. There is wisdom and knowledge that forms the foundations of every decision and action to be taken. Nothing is beyond your comprehension or ability to comfortably handle it. Others seek your council and trust your word, however from your own wealth of experience, you know that they must fathom their own direction, as their circumstances and experiences belong uniquely to them and cannot be resolved based on your personal views or approaches.

In this state of soul alignment, you always work in conjunction with your inner guide, your intuition, in the sure and safe knowledge that you will not be lead along a path that does not serve your highest good or ultimate purpose in being here at this time.

SOUL WHISPERING

Honour your inner wisdom and you will always speak your truth.

*T*his empowered state allows you to confidently draw to you that which you desire. It fuels that glorious 'wind beneath your wings' feeling when your spirit soars and you feel invincible. In this energy you are infinite. You are as your soul intended. This is not the reserved domain of gurus or enlightened ones. It is waiting for you, and you can start to personify your soul within one conscious thought to work with the keys to Soulistic Empowerment.

Resistance means that there is a script of self-limiting fear nibbling away at your determination. These nagging voices are usually those of others, planted within us before we could understand their meaning. When you start to live as your soul intended, you may feel a strange tugging at your heart or a sudden fear arise within you. This is a sign that something ingrained and as yet unchallenged is holding you in your existing mindset, which has ultimately helped create your life to this point. Acknowledge these callings and question their origin. Are they your beliefs, or the beliefs of others based on their reality and experiences. When you have faced these messengers of growth, sift away those that do not reflect or serve your inner knowing and soul's purpose. What you will be left with is the opportunity to strengthen your connection with yourself and your soul journey.

SOUL WHISPERING

Honour your messages from within. Your soul is calling your attention to the next step on the way to happiness and enlightenment.

Overcoming our programming takes recognition of the scripts we are running in the first place. These scripts speak of our self-limiting beliefs, habitual behaviour, ingrained expectations, and unchallenged fears. Notice where, when and how you run them in your daily life. Once you have acknowledged them, you can start to dissolve their impact by consciously letting go of their hold and replacing them with responses and actions that are a reflection of your true self. We need to recognise that the energy of our programmed responses to our desire to be ourselves is not our own, but that of another time, person, or circumstance that has no purpose in the current situation. Recognising that it is possible to balance your personal desires with the responsibilities of life is a key factor to letting go of guilt, self-blame, and limitation.

When we operate as our soul intended, the choices we have to make come easily. Our needs and wants pale in comparison to what serves our joy and contentment in the long term. By attending to our soul's purpose, we follow a path of continual Soulistic Empowerment toward life enrichment.

Take from this potential the fact that you already hold within you everything you need to live the life you were intended to. This is the life you dream of and were meant to live. Employ the principals of Soulistic Empowerment, and your world will become unbelievably abundant as it reflects the authentic you from the inside out.

Life is a song; sing it from your heart.

Life is a dance; feel it in your soul.

Life is a journey; trust it to guide you.

Life is for living, be it.

Life is for loving, share it.

Life is, live it.

Thank you for being part of my journey.

I am delighted that our souls have met again in this lifetime.

Anna-Louise

EPILOGUE

EPILOGUE

$\mathcal{T}$he applause echoed around the exhibition hall, signifying the huge success of my presentation 'Aromatherapy for the Soul', which I gave at the request of the UK's highly regarded Federation of Holistic Therapists, at the Holistic Health Exhibition held in Donington, England in September 2007.

Guiding a mixed audience of over 140 delegates through the Opening Your Heart Healing meditation that is designed to awaken the soul energy and start to heal and harmonise one's life had been ambitious. Trusting my intuition and feeling guided by my inner companion, technical difficulties and the resounding noises from the busy exhibition hall outside our partition walls paled away as we journeyed through the senses and the chakras, using a carefully chosen blend of pure essential oils to anchor the energy.

As I finished, a surge of attendees approached me, wanting to get more involved with this magical process. Their questions and requests duly satisfied, I turned my attention to a man of indefinable age waiting with a younger lady.

As he approached, I sensed a slight recognition, though I could not place the face. I glanced at his name badge, which read simply J. Collinger – Overseas Visitor. His companion's badge was obscured.

This tanned man, who sported a physique that showed that he had been well built in his earlier days, extended his hand, and in a flash my memory recognised him. Joshua! His baritone greeting confirmed my insight, and before I could say anything, he started to tell me what was to be a wonderful story.

'I have been looking forward to meeting you again!' he told me. 'I have wanted to thank you for your guidance all those years ago'.

It had been twenty-four years since I last shook his hand. Without hesitation, he introduced his companion as Laura, his therapist granddaughter who had who trained in aromatherapy when she moved from Canada to London to be with her partner. I had been under the impression that he did not have any family other than his son. Slightly confused, I asked, 'I recall you saying that you only had one son. Is this Carl's daughter?'

His reply did not clarify things immediately. 'She is my daughter's girl', he said. 'Do you remember Sara, to whom you gave a consultation many years ago? She is my daughter from my first marriage when I was very young'.

Now it all tumbled into place. Sara had lost her father when he'd left the family when she was a child. Her deepest wish after loosing her own baby in an accident was to find her father and rebuild their relationship. The key to that was her willingness to forgive him for leaving. Doing so would open the energy highway to allow the contact to be made.

'How on earth did you two meet up?' I asked.

'You gave me a leaflet about a Spiritual Awakening weekend seminar, and I attended it', he explained. 'While I was there, during some of the exercises, we all had to speak about something that we were presently working on within ourselves. Sara spoke about her desire to forgive her father and welcome him back into her life. I listened in stunned silence. As she continued to describe the circumstances that lead to the separation, I realised that I, her father, was sitting not six feet from her.

'I wanted to jump up in the middle of the exercise and hug her and tell her that she had found me. However, I waited until after the end of the weekend because my intuition told me that we were both there for important reasons and that we each needed to get from the weekend what we came for.

'When the seminar was over, as we all said goodbye in the car park, I asked if I could speak with her. I had tried to rehearse what I was going to say, but until I opened my mouth, my mind was swirling with words. Trusting that the right words would come, I found myself starting the introduction by saying, "All weekend, I have had an increasing feeling that we have known each other many years ago". From that moment, the rest was magical. I wish you could have seen the look on her face. We both cried tears of joy, and spent a lovely evening enjoying a nice meal and then watching an amazing thunderstorm over the nearby lake'.

I was stunned but not surprised.

'She told me about you and your guidance, which she felt had brought about this opportunity', he continued. 'Strangely, she wasn't surprised that I knew you too! As we talked, I found a missing piece of my own life puzzle. I told you that I had felt very different since my heart attack, and you had suggested that a new soul had taken over when I had "died". In fact, shortly after I had my consultation with you, I had a dream in which I was told that my new name was Joseph and that this was the name I was to be known by. It felt right, and as I didn't feel like I was living Joshua's life anymore, I changed my name. Sara's face was a mixture of emotions when I told her about my health and new name. When she told me about her lost son, whose name, Joseph, was given to her in a dream, we discovered our true soul family connection.

'It was Laura who spotted your name on the programme of speakers advertised for this exhibition in the *Today's Therapist* magazine. She told her mum, and we have come especially to see you and tell you how everything has worked out'.

Now I was speechless.

Laura came closer and gave me a hug as she said, 'Thank you for helping bring my family back together'.

I told her that I was honoured to have been able to help both her mum and grandfather connect with their inner truth and their souls, and that the rest had been as it was meant to be.

We chatted for a long while. Joseph had followed his dream and moved to Portugal, near his brother, and built a magnificent home to share with Carl when he visited. Sara had adopted two additional children, and they were now in very good careers.

When the time came to say goodbye, I knew that I would never see either of these two special people again. However, the richness of my own journey will always reflect their contribution and, in that way, the connection remains.

On parting, Joseph left me with a huge hug and a thank you that came from the depths of his heart, along with the words: 'The best day of my life will always be the one when I met my precious daughter again. Thank you'.

AFTERWORD

HOW TO BE AS YOUR SOUL

The greatest journey begins with a single step.
— Lao Tzu

*J*ust as the soul is universal, so is the way we can work together. As you continue to travel on your journey, there are many ways by which you can continue to enhance your life though working with your soul potential. I offer a free mentoring service through www.askthesoulwhisperer.com, where you can email your general questions for answering.

I offer one-to-one soul and past life coaching ThetaDNA healing, either in person at my consulting studio or globally, via telephone. For inspirational insights and general soul growth, teleseminars, professional speaking engagements, the transformational '28 Day Soul Coaching and Life Enrichment Programme' as developed by Denise Linn (online or by attending evening classes), soul coaching and life enrichment workshops, plus soul midwifery services (midwife for the dying), guided visualization CD's, and much, much more, which all provide a host of opportunities to help you really live the life you were intended to, visit, www.beasyoursoul.com, www. krisayah.com, or www.anna-louisehaigh.com.

Further general information is available at

www.thesoulwhispererbook.com.

Consulting Studio – By appointment only please

Lavender Court

15 Montpellier Parade

Harrogate

North Yorkshire, England HG1 2TG

++44 (0) 1423 500494

email: *info@anna-louisehaigh.com*

THE SOUL'S FORGIVENESS INTENTION

I embrace all experiences in the knowledge that I attract to myself that which will ensure my growth.

I am willing to hold myself up to the light for purification.

I am willing to forgive myself on all levels, across all lifetimes.

I honour myself and value myself as a person of worth and a much-loved child of the universe.

I forgive (or am willing to think about forgiving) any and all others for their actions.

I release the need to cast blame.

In doing so, I thank any and all others for their willingness to help me grow.

I release myself from self-blame, guilt, and detriment.

I forgive (or am willing to think about forgiving) myself.

I act in grace and integrity as I forgive.

I release the past and move forward richer and more complete.

I forgive, therefore I am free and empowered to live authentically and abundantly in the present moment.

And so it is.

SOUL WHISPERINGS

CHAPTER 1
When Your Soul Calls Your Name

Be ever conscious of each new day.
Add a sprinkle of hope and let your dreams guide your way.

Wisdom involves listening to your heart, speaking with your inner voice, hearing with compassion, and being in touch with your soul.

Nothing is as strong as the spirit – no matter how delicate or colourful the exterior. Think of the fragile butterfly, which can migrate thousands of miles each year.

Live in the knowledge that emergence need not bring emergency.

When your soul rekindles learning from previous lives, the undeniable feelings of 'homecoming' fill your heart and radiate from you in swells of tangible joy.

Take notice of something that catches your eye; you were meant to see it.

Trust in your inner voice. It speaks to you of lifetimes of knowledge gathered specifically to help you in this moment.

CHAPTER 2
Universoul Language

When your soul speaks to you, it guides you with unconditional love toward the next step that is in your highest good. Learn the vocabulary and start to converse fully.

The language of the soul is universal. Listen to your heart and be as your soul.

There is no destination, just the adventure of the journey. If you think you have arrived, you have not begun.

The language of the soul speaks through the heart. It does not require alignment with categories, casts, or cultures.

Honour your journey; it was determined long before you took your first step.

Study your dreams when the night-time calls, and messages from behind the veil will impress upon you.

We come from the light as a divine spark, and we return to the light as a divine spark. It is the journey in between that is enriching.

Turn your eyes skyward and think of home.

Imagine how wonderfully nurturing life will be when you live by the guidance of your soul.

CHAPTER 3

Awakening Your Heart Centres

We are all sparks of divine light radiating from deep within.

When you listen to your heart, your life begins to flow.

There can be journeys within journeys. Watch for the signposts that can lead you much further than you could ever have imagined. Follow your passion for the right reasons. Remember that people matter more than things, and that reality does not have a replay button.

Deep within you are the seeds that create your roots. Cast them carefully. Tend to them lovingly.

As our soul rests in the heart, when we connect with nature, and feel the joy swell within us, we awaken the memory and connection to the source.

To know yourself is to know your soul.

CHAPTER 4

Your Soul Speaks Through Your Health

When you need to know where your life needs healing, look at your health.

Take heed. I, your soul, speak of disharmony in many ways.

When energy accumulates and stagnates, the natural flow of life ceases and challenge steps in.

Honouring the journey of a soul means forgiving ourselves for our humanness.

We are only as strong as our foundations.

When you exercise your creativity, your soul rejoices in celebration.

All that you are and all that you can be is delivered through your soul.

When faced with a challenge, ask yourself, 'If I act out of "love", what would I do in this circumstance?' Your soul will answer through your heart.

Silence is the master of the soul and the mystery of the mind.

I bring wisdom and knowledge. Let yourself benefit from my wisdom. Your life will be richer when you listen to the voice within.

When seeking peace and connection with the divine, look to the heavens through your heart.

CHAPTER 5
The Soul Doctor

Emotions are the energy of life, the creator of oneself, and the healer of the soul.

Free yourself in one act of grace – Forgive.

Your outer reality reflects your choices; your health reflects your inner reality.

Vibrant health is a reflection of one's energetic frequency.

The universe is waiting to share its power and wisdom with you. Just ask, and if it is in your best interest for growth and development, you will receive.

Your soul is ethereal, shapeless, and of gossamer quality. It slips silently between lives, revealing its voice so growth can prevail.

Release the need for control and allow your soul to show you what it feels like to soar.

CHAPTER 6

Finding Inner Peace

Be still and listen. Be still and learn. Be still and be free.

I whisper to you in ways that you would recognize, through something that has meaning to you. Look, listen, feel, and see. It is all there already around you. I always have been.

Inner peace is a state of self-acceptance, self-honouring, forgiveness, and above all self-love.

Forgiveness does not mean that you accept, condone, or welcome the same actions again.

When your soul smiles it lights up the world around you.

My strength is your strength, and your weakness is mine to heal; your turmoil is mine to quell, and your life is mine to enrich.

CHAPTER 7

Sara's Story – The Returnling

Everything happens in Divinely right timing.

To connect with your soul, be still and listen to the wisdom that radiates from your heart. It knows your truth and will always guide you for your best interests. The secret is to be still and listen, and then to have the courage to trust and act on the messages you receive.

What we think about most, we attract to ourselves.

CHAPTER 8

Love — Your Soul's Greatest Quest

With love, anything is possible. Start with your dreams.

The language of your heart is universal. Listen to your heart and be as your soul.

We attract that which mirrors our inner beliefs about ourselves. Be sure to radiate your most positive qualities, as this will act as a beam and draw those who genuinely recognise these higher qualities in themselves.

When something or someone challenges you, you are being given an opportunity to grow. Seize it, and embrace the lesson, and this will soon let other opportunities follow.

Because we are all souls here on Earth to learn, do not be too hard on yourself. Life can be challenging enough on its own without adding to it with self-criticism.

When we look outside ourselves for love and validation of who we are, we silence our own ability to love ourselves unconditionally. Therefore, we allow others to control how we feel about ourselves, which can only ever be a reflection of how they feel about themselves.

CHAPTER 9
Discovering Your Soul's Purpose

When you are in harmony with your soul, you awaken within you the world of infinite possibilities that is your birthright.

The tools to carve the life you were meant to live are always in reach. Take time to learn how to use them skillfully, and your reward will be a masterpiece.

Trust as you progress. You are always supported, guided, and cared for unconditionally.

When you find yourself drawn to something that is out of the normal range of your interests or habits, take note, because the universe won't let an opportunity go by you if it is meant for you. Take action the first time you get the nudge and follow your instincts.

CHAPTER 10

How to Hear the Voice of Your Soul

Listen to the stillness of the morning mists; they speak of the promise of the day.

Know that we have a connection, and that this will always be true. I am here to guide your life, and in return, to learn from you.

There are opportunities everywhere. Be open and willing to experience new challenges, and your world will be a very magical and rich place.

CHAPTER 11

Living Your Dreams

You already have everything within you to achieve what you desire. You are everything.

The excitement you feel swelling up from within is coming from your soul, as you unite with the infinite within you.

At the point when you see the only option as retreat, you are at the crest of an amazing leap forward. Seize it, embrace it, take that risk, and be thankful that your soul held the vision to guide you to this crucial moment.

CHAPTER 12

Soulistic Empowerment

When the moment arrives, spread your wings and take flight.

Sip slowly at the source that nourishes your soul. Although endless, it is worth savouring.

When challenges face you, remember that there is learning to be gained. Learn the lesson, and you can move on.

Deep within us is a spiritual anchor that holds us fast as we test how far the chain of life's opportunities will let us venture from our chosen, original mooring.

In these times of accelerated spiritual awakening, there may be days when you think you may never reach a certain level of understanding, or inner connection. Do not measure yourself against others. You are not living their life or travelling their journey. We each have our own unique contributions to make. You are leaving the footprints of your soul in the sands of time. Dance on!

Honour your inner wisdom and you will always speak your truth.

Honour your messages from within. Your soul is calling your attention to the next step on the way to happiness and enlightenment.

OTHER BOOKS FROM LIFESUCCESS PUBLISHING

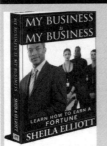

MY BUSINESS IS MY BUSINESS

Learn How to Earn a Fortune

Shelia Elliott

ISBN 978-1-59930-149-5

WE THE NEW ME

Unleash the Creative Power of Your Mind

Debbii McKoy

ISBN 978-159930104-4

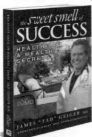

THE SWEET SMELL OF SUCCESS

Health & Wealth Secrets

James "Tad" Geiger M.D.

ISBN 978-1-59930-088-7

SEX

Do You Want More?

Linda Wilde

ISBN 978-1-59930-160-0

WEALTH MATTERS

Abundance is Your Birthright

Chris J. Snook with Chet Snook

ISBN 978-1-59930-096-2

THE SUCCESS TOOLBOX

For Entrepreneurs

Janis Vos

ISBN 978-1-59930-005-4

GET THE RENOVATION YOU REALLY WANT!

Renovating your home should be a wonderful experience...

John Salton

ISBN 978-1-59930-169-3

THE GIRLZ GUIDE TO BUILDING WEALTH

...and men like it too

Maya Galletta, Aaron Cohen, Polly McCormick, Mike McCormick

ISBN 978-1-59930-048-1